HILL WALKING IN DORSET

CIRCULAR WALKS TO TWENTY OF DORSET'S HIGHEST PEAKS

BY
EDWARD R GRIFFITHS

ALSO IN THE GREEN FIELDS BOOKS SERIES

THE STOUR VALLEY PATH   ISBN 0 9519376 7 7
LONG-DISTANCE PATH
(FULLY REVISED EDITION)

"...the book is a gem which anybody...will add quickly and gratefully to their bookshelf' .....Dorset Life

THE CRANBORNE CHASE PATH   ISBN 0 9519376 2 6
LONG-DISTANCE PATH

"....combining exciting local colour with meticulous route information".....Greenlink Countryside Guide

"....the anecdotes and passionate descriptions will delight even those familiar with the Chase".....Western Gazette

THE BLACKMORE VALE PATH   ISBN 0 9519376 3 4
LONG-DISTANCE PATH

"....a walk to be savoured.   Happy rambling and enjoy Dorset".....Blackmore Vale Magazine

DORSET IN A FORTNIGHT   ISBN 0 9519376 4 2
CIRCULAR WALKS

"...reflects the diversity of landscape and beauty of the county....you won't be disappointed".....Country Walking

RAMBLES FROM DORSET TOWN   ISBN 0 9519376 5 0
CIRCULAR WALKS

ISBN 0 9530338 0 5

Published by Green Fields Books
13 Dalewood Avenue, Bear Cross
Bournemouth, BH11 9NR

CONTENTS

BIBLIOGRAPHY

History and Antiquities of the County of Dorset: Rev John Hutchins 1861-64 edition
Inventory of Historical Monuments in the County of Dorset - H.M.S.O. 1970
Inside Dorset: Monica Hutchings
Portrait of Dorset: Ralph Whiteman - Robert Hale, London
Literary Guide to the British Isles: Dorothy Eagle and Hilary Carnel - Ox. Univ. Press
William Wordsworth: Hunter Davies - Hamlyn Paperbacks

INTRODUCTION

Scattered about the beautiful county of Dorset there are many small mountains, the ascents of which are not the most difficult in the world. However, when conquered, they offer stupendous views and a fair sense of achievement.

I know you've been to the Lake District and climbed some of England's most challenging mountains (So have I) but, just because you live in Dorset - or are only visiting - it doesn't mean you can't climb some rewarding peaks. If you climb all of the hills contained in this book, you will have climbed the equivalent of 3 Scafell Pikes (3210ft, starting at the usual mecca of Seathwaite Farm at 422ft with a height gain of 2788ft). Better than that, you will have visited some of Dorset's hidden villages on your way to these scattered peaks and enjoyed some of the loveliest scenery anywhere in the country. Even Alfred Wainwright enjoyed the lower hills of the Northern Lakes - and you can't just pop up to the Lake District every day, can you?

The chosen hills for your delectation are - in order of peak heights IN FEET:

HILL	HT ABOVE SEA LEVEL	START AND HT	GAIN
PILSDON PEN and	911	Broadwindsor 497	414
LEWESDON HILL	895	Wall Farm 658	237
MELBURY BEACON	865	Compton Abbas 352	513
BELL HILL via	849	Turnworth Road 500	349
OKEFORD HILL	773	Okeford Fitzpaine 247	526
LAMBERT'S CASTLE	842	Wootton Fitzpaine 197	645
BLACKDOWN HILL	784	Portesham 227 via Black Down Barn 500	670
DUNCLIFFE HILL	691	New Gate Farm 283	408
SWYRE HEAD	666	Kimmeridge Bay 55	611
GODLINGSTON HILL	654	Ulwell Lay-by 120	534
and BALLARD DOWN	545	Ulwell crossing 197	348
HAMBLEDON HILL	623	Child Okeford 197	426
GOLDEN CAP	618	Seatown 33	585
PENTRIDGE HILL	608	Pentridge 279	329
WHITEWAY HILL and	608	Worbarrow Bay 50	558
TYNEHAM CAP	530	Tyneham 148	382
GERRARD'S HILL	572	Beaminster 164	408

HILL (HIGHEST FIRST)	HT ABOVE SEA LEVEL	START AND HT	GAIN
EAST HILL via	519	White Horse 434	85
WHITE HORSE HILL	434	Sutton Poyntz 53	381
CHAPEL HILL	250	Fleet Car Park 49	201

Clearly, this is not an exhaustive list of the highest peaks in Dorset - just some of those with good, circular walking access   I have tried to find the lowest possible starting points not too far from the hills but far enough to give you a sense of anticipation before you begin the ascents - and a circular walk if possible.

TOTAL HEIGHT OF THESE 20 HILLS ABOVE SEA LEVEL IS 13237 FT AND OVERALL HEIGHT GAIN IS 8610 FT   Equivalent to 3.09 Scafell Pikes (3210ft) assuming a height gain of 2788ft each time if starting at Seathwaite Farm (422ft).

DISTRIBUTION:

HILL	HEIGHT	GAIN

NORTH:

HILL	HEIGHT	GAIN
Melbury Beacon.	865	513
Okeford Hill and Bell Hill	773 and 849	875
Duncliffe Hill	691	408
Hambledon Hill	623	426
		TOTAL 2222

SOUTH:

HILL	HEIGHT	GAIN
Black Down Hill	784	670
Swyre Head	666	611
Godlingston Hill and	654 and 545	
Ballard Down		882
Whiteway Hill and	608	
Tyneham Cap	530	940
White Horse Hill and	434 and 519	
East Hill		466
Chapel Hill	250	201
		TOTAL 3770

EAST:

HILL	HEIGHT	GAIN
Pentridge Hill	608	329
		TOTAL 329

WEST:

HILL	HEIGHT	GAIN
Pilsdon Pen and	911 and 895	
Lewesdon Hill		651
Lambert's Hill	842	645
Golden Cap	618	585
Gerrard's Hill	572	408
		TOTAL 2289

So, if you plan it right, you can BAG all of each area's peaks in a period of days (or hours) to suit your own ambitions - but don't forget the walks to get there and back and the travelling distances between each hill.   Each hill is shown on the Location Map below together with its O.S. map reference.   None of these is a particularly long walk but each one is particularly fine and the views are all completely enchanting.

LOCATION MAP AND MILEAGES IN BRACKETS:

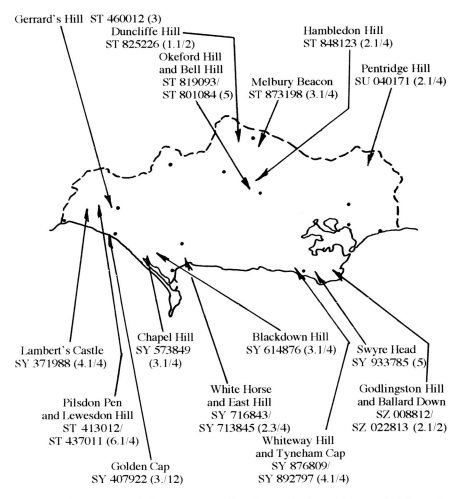

Gerrard's Hill ST 460012 (3)

Duncliffe Hill
ST 825226 (1.1/2)

Okeford Hill
and Bell Hill
ST 819093/
ST 801084 (5)

Hambledon Hill
ST 848123 (2.1/4)

Pentridge Hill
SU 040171 (2.1/4)

Melbury Beacon
ST 873198 (3.1/4)

Lambert's Castle
SY 371988 (4.1/4)

Chapel Hill
SY 573849
(3.1/4)

Blackdown Hill
SY 614876 (3.1/4)

Swyre Head
SY 933785 (5)

Pilsdon Pen
and Lewesdon Hill
ST 413012/
ST 437011 (6.1/4)

White Horse
and East Hill
SY 716843/
SY 713845 (2.3/4)

Godlingston Hill
and Ballard Down
SZ 008812/
SZ 022813 (2.1/2)

Golden Cap
SY 407922 (3./12)

Whiteway Hill
and Tyneham Cap
SY 876809/
SY 892797 (4.1/4)

Just one other comment before you start. I've been asked to point out that the only comparisons between these hills and Scafell Pike are the accumulated heights and, just because you have successfully climbed all of these Dorset peaks, it doesn't mean you can tackle Scafell Pike with the same equipment and joie de vivre.   Its boulder fields, its high rocky scrambles in the mist and its possibilities of damaging your bodily parts all demand a different preparation and fitness altogether.   I know it's obvious to you but it's best to make these things perfectly clear, isn't it?

VIEWS AND INFORMATION

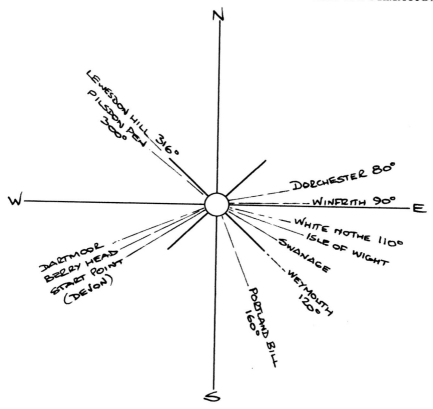

PORTESHAM:

The village lies to the South of a long chalk ridge which is topped with gravel.   This is excellent grazing land but is cultivated only where it could be levelled - and it has been since Neolithic times.   The Parish Church of St Peter is built of Portland rubble stone and the 12thC nave still stands.   The Tower is 13thC and the building escaped the usual Victorian 'improvements'.

THE HARDY MONUMENT:

Arthur Dyke Troyte designed this octagonal stone tower which was built just five years after Hardy's death in 1939.   The foundation stone was laid on October 21st 1844 by Henry Goddard of Bridport, the contractor.   It is 70 ft high and restoration isn't exactly a regular occurrence.   It was restored in 1908 but not substantially since then until 1996-97.

Thomas Masterman Hardy was Nelson's flag-captain during the Battle of Trafalgar and it is in his arms that Nelson died.   He also later became an Admiral and served the Navy with much distinction.

1 - BLACKDOWN HILL   784 FEET

O.S. MAP NO. 194   REFERENCE SY 614876

The monument to Admiral Sir Thomas Masterman Hardy (erected in 1844) standing on top of Blackdown Hill is a landmark which is visible for miles around.   Base camp is at Portesham which lies on the B3157 Abbotsbury to Weymouth road. Southern National bus 210 calls there, as do local services 6, 60, 61 and 63.   The walk is often steep with fine views over downland with grazing sheep and through pine woods.

Start at the junction of the B3157 with the Dorchester turning. Walk up Front Street past Church Lane and the school on your left and up past St Peter's.   Pass Winters Lane on your right and bend right by the Post Office with Back Street on your left. Follow Front Street up to a right Bridleway/track between gardens, signposted 'Hardy Monument 1.1/2'.   Follow it around a left bend into a tree-lined track which rises to a Footpath and Bridleway-signed gate onto the steep downs of Portesham Hill.

Follow the grassy slope very steeply uphill and close to the hawthorns near the LH broken stone wall.   Following the broken wall, bend round to the right until you reach a gate in the very top corner.   Turn left through the gate and walk up, past two Bridleway arrows on your left.   Follow the RH wall around to the right and, at the next gate, you have reached a height of 613 ft.   Go through the gate and follow the RH fence/wall down to another Bridleway-arrowed gate by a small pine wood. Through the gate, turn left down a stony track with a fence on your right.   Follow it down to another gate before Blackdown Barn. You have now dropped back to 500 ft. The track bends left but keep over to the RH fence, past a gate and a 'Bridleway to Coast Path' sign, up onto a narrow flinty path.   With a broken wall on your right and pine woods on your left, keep going up.   Soon, cross a level, grassy woodland track and keep climbing on the narrow Bridle path with trees on both sides.   Eventually, you emerge onto a second woodland track.   Keep straight on, past a path which drops down on your right, and follow it round a long Z-bend.   After 100 yards, the path comes back out from your right.   Turn left here and climb up a flinty path onto a ridge of gorse and bracken.   The path continues up and over this ridge but turn left again onto an eroded gravel and flint path and climb up steeply through pines at first. Emerging onto the open hill of gorse and bracken, you can see the Hardy Monument. Follow the path up, around the edge of an old stone quarry onto the parking area.

Savour the views for as long as you like and then look for the way down.   Go across the car park to the RH edge of the quarry.   Look across the bracken to your right for a milestone on a grassy path.   That is where you want so choose a suitable path and head for it.   At the stone, signed 'Inland Route West Bexington', turn left and follow the path down into a mixed beech and pine wood.   The path widens and passes a right turning path and two grassy woodland tracks to the left.   After 1/2 mile, emerging from the trees, go through two upright posts across a ditch and turn left onto a grass track which comes from a field gate over on your right.   You've been here before, so just follow the track past Blackdown Barn, up the other side of the valley and straight past the gate by the small pine wood where you arrived earlier.   Keep to this grassy and stony track up and over the crest of the hill and down past Portesham Farm.   Go over the cattle grid where a RH Footpath turns off over excavations in the hillside and keep to the descending tarmac track, past a RH limestone quarry and all the way to another cattle grid onto a road.   This is a very pleasant descent with time to admire the super views over the Chesil Beach and out to sea.   Finally follow Winters Lane down past houses on either side and back into Front Street, Portesham.

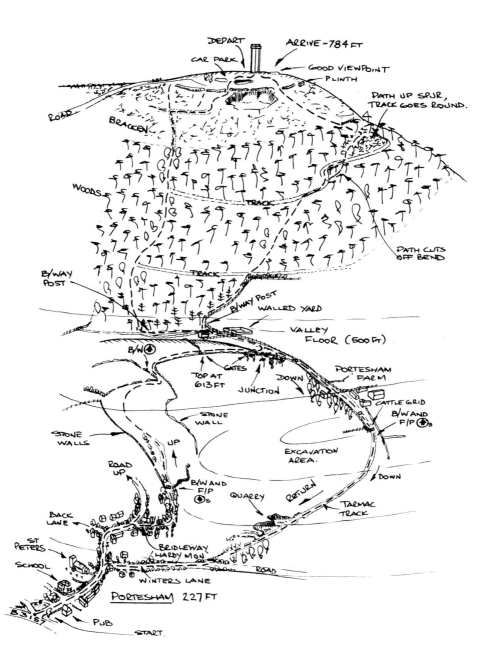

O.S. MAP NO. 194   REFERENCE SY 573849

The stone and mostly thatched village of Abbotsbury is on the B3157 Bridport to Weymouth coast road between the unique Chesil Beach and the ridge which carries the Dorset Coast Path.   Local buses 60, 61 and 63 run here as does the Southern National 210.   Parking is easy and this walk begins, for its proximity to sea level, at the Fleet Car Park by Abbotsbury sub-tropical gardens (The Fleet is the stretch of water between the mainland and Chesil Beach).   It is a particularly pleasant stroll and can be achieved quite easily.   In fact, you may be in the minority if you're wearing boots.

Begin by going over the little bridge to the left of the conveniences and turning left onto the lane between the tamarisk hedge and the beach.   Just before a path turns off into 'Fleet Nature Reserve', there is a brief glimpse of St Catherine's Chapel across the lynchets in the field over the hedge on your left.   At the Coast Path stone to the 'Swannery 1.1/4', go through a gate onto a fenced track.   Around a long sweeping LH bend, cross a small bridge over a stream on your right and go over a stile into the field.   Follow its RH wire fence over a hump and stroll down to the far RH corner.

Go over the stile between the dry-stone wall and the gate and then over the next stile into another long field with a RH wire fence.   Follow the level path towards the far RH corner, with the reed beds of the Nature Reserve over on your right.   Turn left at the end of this field and follow the stone wall up to a stile which leads into another field with a RH banked hedge.   With a small wood and the drive to the Swannery over on your right, keep going along the RH edge of the field, bearing left as you go.   Go over the low ridge of an old field hedge and turn left towards Chapel Hill.   On the hill, there is a 'Permissive Path' stile in the wire fence.   Over the stile, follow the direction of the stone sign - straight up the steep banks and slipping topsoil of the hill to another stile in the wire fence which comes up from the woods on your right.

Go over the stile and keep on up the steepest part of the hill.   Nearing the top, cross a narrow dyke and a green track coming from your left.   Cross the hill to the massive structure of St Catherine's Chapel.   Have a good look around the Chapel and enjoy the views.   This is where you'll meet people in trainers and high-heeled shoes who have climbed their first and only hill because it's there and they're on holiday. They'll have come up from Abbotsbury and I'm sure you will soon spot the wide grassy track which retreats downhill from the corner of the Chapel's wire fence.

With good views over the village to the church and the tithe barn, stroll down the grass thoroughfare, past kissing gates in the stone wall near the bottom and round to the left where the more distinct farm track runs down past the stone farm buildings to a gate in the bottom corner.   Go through the kissing gate and turn left onto the level, banked and hedged track.   Follow the track, past a RH turning with a Footpath arrow on the far corner and on past 'Smugglers'.   With a steep LH bank, the track drops down through a gate onto another main track with Footpath and Bridleway arrows on the left corner post.   Turn left and follow the track down, passing gates on either side, until you have a stream as company on your left.   Recognise it?   It soon runs under a bridge before the gate where you turned off this same track earlier.

Pass the bridge and keep straight on back to the Fleet Car Park.   I hope you enjoyed this easy walk for its pleasant fields, the fine views over the Chesil Beach and Abbotsbury village and the tremendous structure of St Catherine's Chapel itself.

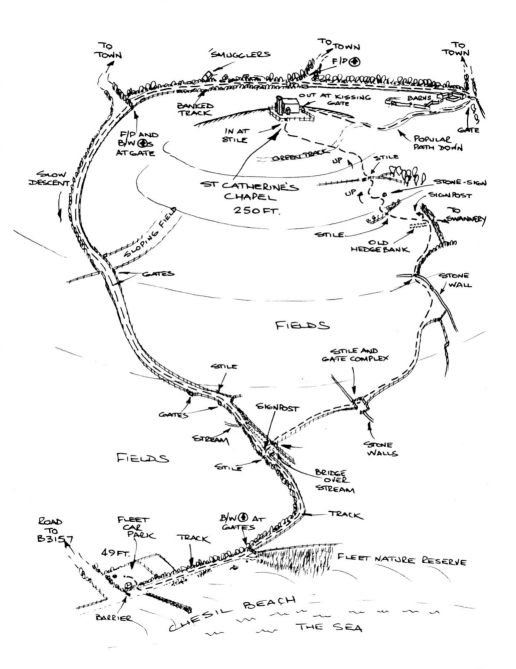

VIEWS AND INFORMATION

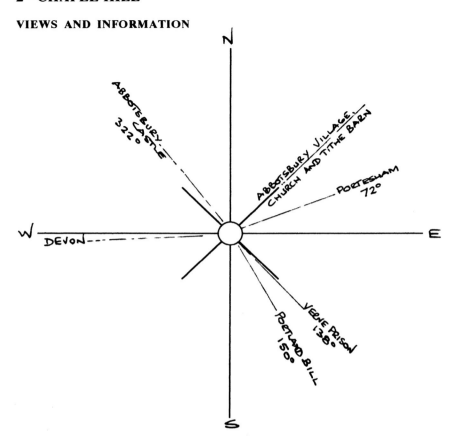

ST CATHERINE'S CHAPEL:

This massive structure, is 42 ft long by 15 ft wide inside, heavily buttressed with 4 ft thick sandstone walls, was built either during the time of Abbot Henry de Thorpe who died in 1376 or Abbot William Cerne who ruled the Abbey between 1376 and 1401. At the Dissolution of the Monasteries of 1536-39, it wasn't destroyed because of its conspicuous use to sailors (of all faiths) as a landmark.   It is dedicated to St Catherine, a high-born scholarly lady of Alexandria in Egypt.   For her faith, she was tortured on a wheel and then beheaded in 290AD in the reign of Emperor Maximinus.

THE FLEET AND ABBOTSBURY:

The long narrow channel of sea-water which is trapped between the Chesil Beach and the mainland, runs from the Portland causeway to the Nature Reserve.   It was used for testing Barnes Wallis' bouncing bombs.   St Nicholas' Church was built between the 15thC and 16thC but it was much restored in 1807-08 when the gallery was added. Two holes in the back of the pulpit's sounding board are said to have been caused by musket shot during the civil war.   The ancient tithe barn which still retains half of its thatch was built about 1400.

The Rev Hutchins in his 'History and Antiquities of the County of Dorset' says of Duncliffe Hill: "On the top of a high hill in this parish called Dunkly or Duncliff hill, rises a perpetual spring. It is about a mile West of Shaftesbury and has a circular entrenchment on the top". I'm afraid I found neither the spring nor the entrenchment. Maybe the planting operations have obscured the latter and the trees themselves take all of the spring water - or maybe I didn't look hard enough.

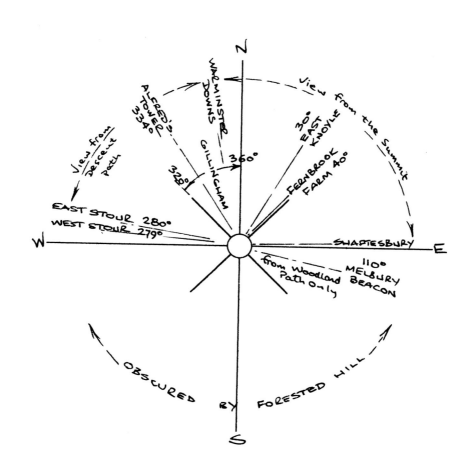

3 - DUNCLIFFE HILL   691 FEET

O.S. MAP NO. 183   REFERENCE ST 825226

Duncliffe Hill is unique in the Blackmore Vale in that, wherever you go, it is almost always visible.   Although it isn't very far from the high, steep Western escarpment of Cranborne Chase, it stands proud and aloof with its ever-present crown of trees.

Duncliffe Hill's sheer presence makes its conquest a necessity but it is generous in the gifts it bestows on those who make the pilgrimage to its inviting slopes.   Here are lush green fields, wind swept forest walks, the cries of crows and the twitter of all manner of birds.   There is the smell of warm resin in the summer and of damp, fresh air in the autumn.   There are surprising views through the trees whilst an awakening wood in spring is glorious anywhere.   Surrounded by farmland, access to Duncliffe Hill is best begun on the lane which runs from the A30 Sherborne Causeway from Shaftesbury to Stour Row.   About 1 mile after turning off the Causeway at the sign for 'Stour Row', a wide gravel track turns left just after the RH turn at New Gate Farm.   There is room to park a couple of cars if you're thoughtful.

Go through the gate marked 'No entry for Vehicles' and walk along the 500 yards of gravel track, first with an oak and ash avenue and, through the next gate, along the RH edge of a hedged field.   Arriving at Duncliffe Wood, the 'Woodland Trust' welcomes you as you pass through a wicket gate onto a narrower, rising gravel track. Ignore the turnings to right and left until you reach the brow of the hill with a wide area on your left and views ahead towards Melbury Beacon if you were to continue. Don't! Turn left here, through a wooden barrier with a notice prohibiting horses - thank goodness for a safe path.

Go up the narrow grassy path, through more barriers, and up and up to a right branch. Keep turning left though and follow the path to another barrier at a crossing of paths. Take note of the LH descending path - that's your return route - but turn right and keep climbing.   Pass a bank and ditch on the RH edge of a steep slope and then follow the sometimes stepped path along a narrow ridge.   At a wicket gate, you emerge into the sunlight where the O.S. trig point stands at 691 feet on the grassy top of Duncliffe Hill amongst bracken and brambles.   Just past the concrete block, you will have views of the high Warminster Downs away to the left whilst the red-roofed village is East Knoyle.   Below you, the prominent farm is Fernbrook Farm with the walled Motcombe Kennels beyond it.

Now, return to the cross-paths and keep straight down - becoming grassy again. There are more clay steps as you reach a wicket gate which lets you out of the woods, past a LH turning grassy path, and into a steeply sloping field.   There are better views from here than from the top.   There are super views over Gillingham to Warminster Downs whilst, swinging anti-clockwise, you will see Alfred's Tower on the ridge overlooking Stourhead in Wiltshire.   Descending the field, you bear left along the fence and then the bumpy hill that you can see about 3/4 mile away is East Stour Common.   A little further round, you will see the church at East Stour with West Stour and the Ship Inn slightly beyond it to its left.

Keep on down, following the fence, until you find a hedge where you turn left (South) and go through the gate with Bridleway arrows.   Now level, keep following the edge of the wood and go through the gate/gap in the next hedge.   Recognising where you are, keep straight on to the gravel track and turn right - back to the parking area.

1 2

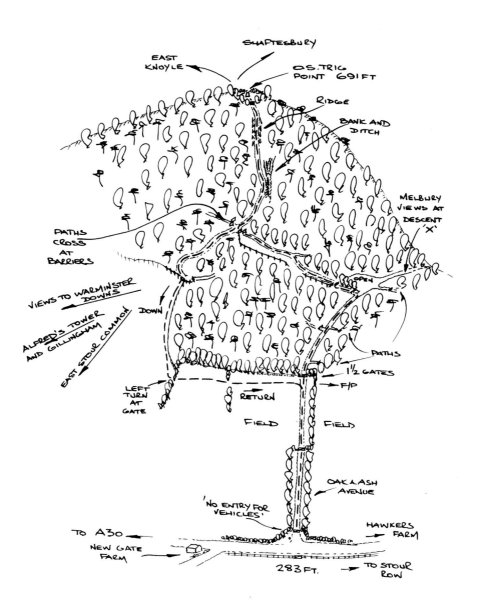

SHAFTESBURY

EAST KNOYLE

O.S. TRIG POINT 691 FT

RIDGE

BANK AND DITCH

MELBURY VIEWS AT DESCENT 'X'

PATHS CROSS AT BARRIERS

VIEWS TO WARMINSTER DOWNS

ALFRED'S TOWER AND GILLINGHAM COMMON

DOWN

EAST STOUR COMMON

OPEN

PATHS

1½ GATES

F/P

LEFT TURN AT GATE

RETURN

FIELD

FIELD

OAK & ASH AVENUE

'NO ENTRY FOR VEHICLES'

TO A30

HAWKERS FARM

NEW GATE FARM

283 FT.

TO STOUR ROW

4 - GERRARD'S HILL 572 FEET

O.S. MAP NO. 193 REFERENCE ST 460012

Beaminster is on the A3066 Bridport to Crewkerne road and this walk starts in Church Street, just off the market square. The old stone cottages in the back streets are very pretty and well worth a closer look, either before or after the walk. Gerrard's Hill boasts a very steep final assault with superb views on the way whilst the approach and return offer most enjoyable walking on grass and through an ancient wood.

In Church Street, walk past St Mary's with its most impressive tower and keep straight on along Shorts Lane. Go along a banked, stony path to a right-turning track by a stile and gate with Bridleway and Footpath arrows. Cross the long meadow with a stream down on your left and houses over on your right. At the end, go over a Wessex Ridgeway and Footpath-arrowed stile into the lane and turn left. Cross the bridge and turn first right at a gate with Footpath and W/R arrows. After 100 yards, turn left at a gate between a LH hedge and a RH tarmac yard (with Footpath arrow). At the end of the short path, go over another stile. (There are so many arrows on this walk, I won't mention any more unless they're important). Bear half-right and aim diagonally up the hill for a squeeze-stile to the right of a stone barn. Turn left around the far end of the barn and follow the path up and over the crest of the hill to a double stile through a deep hedge. Descend to a stile in the wire fence - *and stop*. Before you go down through new trees to the gap in the facing hedge, look down to your left where the hedges converge into a gap in the corner. You will be going through there on your return, so make a mental note. Now, go through the gap and descend through more young trees to another double stile with a bridge over the stream in the hedge. Over this bridge, look up the hill facing you. There is a tree half-way up with a Footpath arrow post to its right. Climb up slowly and with plenty of stops.

Past the tree, keep going slowly up (at 280 degrees WNW) until you find a stile next to a gate in the top corner of the field. Climb over the stile, cross the track with a RH gate and go over the opposite stile onto the fine-turfed slopes of Gerrard's Hill. Follow the old RH hedge until it veers off on a level contour. Then keep climbing on the grassy path, aiming for the beech clump on the top. The O.S. trig point is just left before the trees whilst the path goes right past the trees for views Westward.

Returning to that gap in the earlier hedge, turn right through the gap. Leave the field (no arrows) onto a green path with trees of the Woodland Trust on your right and a hedge on your left. Continue to a squeeze-stile and follow the short track to the road with a Footpath arrow on your left. Cross the road onto the concrete track/Bridleway for 'Knowle Farm' and follow it to a collection of barns. Turn left up the rising track (no arrows) to a T-junction at the top. A Footpath arrow points right but turn left, through a gate onto a gravel track. Just before the track turns sharp right, go through the LH gate with the Footpath arrow into a rising field.

Follow the LH hedge up to a gate and stile which lead to a descending grass track but stay in the field and turn right alongside the top hedge. At the top, go through the kissing gate into a beautiful old wood, mostly of beech, oak and sycamore, on a steep RH slope. Follow the undulating main path to the far end and descend the steps to another kissing gate. Through the gate, turn half-left and follow the popular path down diagonally to join the gravel track at the bottom by a Bridleway arrow post. Follow the track, through another kissing gate and down a cottage-lined track back into St Mary's Well Street and Church Street where you began.

1 4

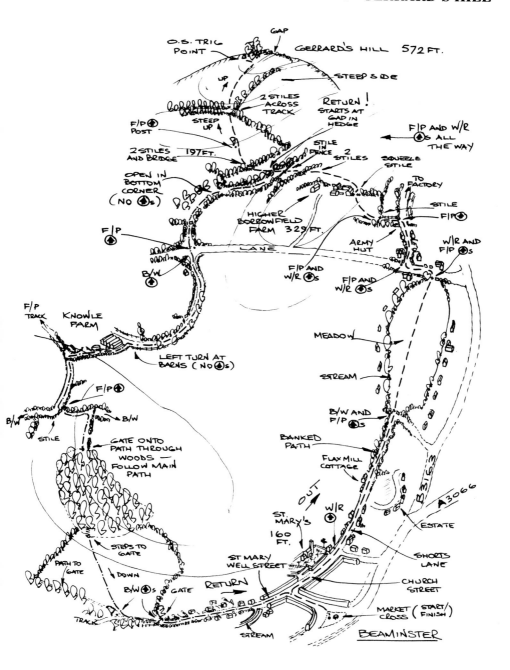

4 - GERRARD'S HILL

VIEWS AND INFORMATION

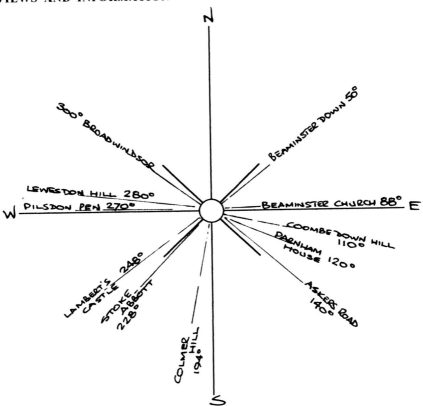

N

300° BROADWINDSOR

BEAMINSTER DOWN 50°

LEWESDON HILL 280°

PILSDON PEN 270°

W

BEAMINSTER CHURCH 88° E

COOMBE DOWN HILL 110°

PARNHAM HOUSE 120°

LAMBERT'S CASTLE 248°

STOKE ABBOTT 228°

ASKER ROAD 140°

COLMER HILL 194°

S

BEAMINSTER:
"This was the ancient capital of a hundred to which it gave its name" - Hutchins.   Its importance translated later into the magnificence of the sandstone Church of the Nativity of the Blessed Virgin Mary with its tower which was built in 1520.   The list of chaplains goes back to William Vale 1408 - about the time that the present church was built.   Beaminster (or Beiminstre in the Domesday Book) has had more than its fair share of conflagrations.   Apart from the East Street and part of Church Street, it was almost completely destroyed by a fire which was begun by the discharging of a musket in a house gable during the Civil War on 14th April 1644.   A similar catastrophe struck on 28th June 1684 and again on 31st March 1781.   Much of the town's wealth was based on flax and there was a mill by the River Brit at Slape.

GERRARD'S HILL:
John Gerard was the builder of the first Parnham House in about 1400.   Robert Strode rebuilt it in the mid 16thC.   Altered by George Strode altered the mainly Tudor house, which may be seen from the hill but not from the main road, at it was remodelled by John Nash for the Oglander family in 1810.   There is also a Gerrard's Green nearby.

INFORMATION AND VIEWS FROM GODLINGSTON HILL

GODLINGSTON:

Godlingston and Moleham were separate entries in the Domesday Book but Moleham is now just a parcel of land to the South of Godlingston Farm. It was held by Durandus the carpenter, a servant of the King, together with some land at Wilkswood. From the Talbot family of Henry II and Edward I's times, the land passed to Robert Rempston and the manor house was built around this time. The deeds date back to 1427 and the house and lands belonged to the Mompessons of Langton Matravers in the 15thC and 16thC. The house has a very thick-walled stone tower at its West end (probably for defensive purposes) and it originally had a high - up to the roof - main hall. It was greatly rebuilt in the 17thC when an upper floor was added and, following a fire in the 19thC, the inside was much altered.

The Nine Barrow Down Ridge - and the Worth Matravers and Langton Matravers ridge on the opposite side of the Swanage to Corfe Castle road - was used during the War for RADAR development and strange aerials still stand near the O.S. trig point on this side. I'm sure they're nothing sinister, though.

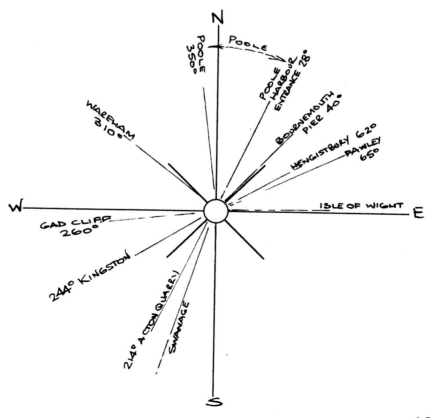

5 - GODLINGSTON HILL AND BALLARD DOWN 654 FEET/ 545 FEET

O.S. MAP NO. 195   REFERENCE SZ 008812/022813

STAGE 1 - GODLINGSTON HILL

There is a Wilts and Dorset bus stop for the No 150 bus at Ulwell, just down the road from a pair of lay-bys on the East side of the Swanage to Studland road.   However you arrive, the walk to these two peaks begins in the first lay-by.   Godlingston Hill lies above one of the gaps in the long chalk ridge which runs from Worbarrow Bay to Old Harry Rocks.   The ridge to the West of Godlingston Hill is Nine Barrow Down and forms a superb walk to Corfe Castle which guards the next gap along.   The ridge to the East - to Old Harry Rocks - is Ballard Down and is your second destination today.

From the lay-by, cross over to the other side of the road and follow the pavement.   It runs out at a stile with a Footpath arrow in the LH hedge.   Go over the stile and follow the well-used path around the slopes of Round Down, almost parallel with the road but ascending slightly away from it.   At a kissing gate which leads into Ulwell Caravan Park, bear right to follow the National Trust stone direction for 'Corfe Castle 3.3/4'. Follow the long, ascending path to a LH farm gate where a chalk track runs up and over a nearby ridge between two small quarries.

Keep following the fence, noting the change in soil if the field over your fence is ploughed.   The higher slopes are clearly chalk whilst the lower slopes are reddish Wealden clay.   That's why there is a small brick factory down at the bottom of this field.   The clay is perfect for building bricks.   Now, go up and over a small narrow ridge and drop down onto the chalk track which comes up from your right.   Make a note of this track because that is the way down to the start of the Ballard Down walk.

For now, follow the chalk track uphill and, when you meet the N.T. stone offering alternative routes (to Corfe Castle), take the upper track, signed 'Ridge Path 3.1/4'. There are good views over to Swanage which allow you good reasons to take it easy on the long, steady climb.   As the track becomes more rocky, keep ascending and go through the gate with the N.T. 'Godlingston Hill' sign and continue your climb on the fence-enclosed track.   Soon, the track widens out into a high field and dissolves into grass before continuing just below the ridge of Nine Barrow Down.   The RH fence runs up the hill, protecting the installation of aerials on your right.

For today's purposes, walk diagonally away from this RH fence to find the O.S trig point on the highest point of Nine Barrow Down.   The views are terrific from here and should be savoured but before too long you have to return to the bottom of Godlingston Hill for your connection for Ballard Down.

Arriving back at the T-junction of chalk paths, keep on down by keeping Round Down on your right and the valley floor of Giant's Trencher on your left.   When you see a gate at the end of the track, bear diagonally left and aim for the far corner of the roadside wire fence.   (A line aiming for the erosion on the opposite hill is a good direction to take).   In the corner, you will find a stile with a N.T. stone pointing back to Nine Barrow Down and Corfe Castle.   Climb over into the road and cross carefully into a grassy area opposite where you will find another stile with a Footpath arrow pointing sharp right.   This only leads back to the lay-by so look up and follow the steep, eroded path instead.   You wanted hill walks, didn't you?

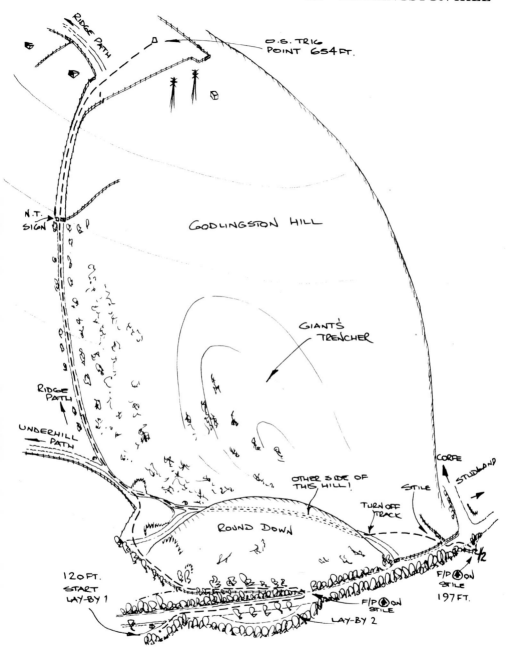

RIDGE PATH

O.S. TRIG
POINT 654 FT.

N.T.
SIGN

GODLINGSTON HILL

GIANT'S
TRENCHER

RIDGE
PATH

UNDERHILL
PATH

OTHER SIDE OF
THIS HILL!

CORFE

STUDLAND

STILE

TURN OFF
TRACK

ROUND DOWN

120 FT.
START
LAY-BY 1

F/P ON
STILE

LAY-BY 2

F/P ON
STILE

197 FT.

STAGE 2 - BALLARD DOWN OBELISK

This really is a steep climb and you should stop frequently on the way up to look for the National Trust's Spyway Barn. This will appear on the distant ridge beyond the chalk tracks' junction between Round Down and Godlingston Hill somewhere on your ascent - but you'll have to stop quite often to search it out.

Keep close to the gorse bushes on your right as you scramble up this hill and, when the eroded chalk path ends near the top, keep on climbing on grass towards a gate and stile which crosses the ridge end. Over the stile, keep following the LH fence until it reaches a pair of gates that open onto a chalk/grass track which comes up from the Studland road near Dean Hill and the Golf Course.

Turn right onto the track and follow it as it veers round to the left, now becoming just a gentle slope. Go through the small gate into a wide area with the obelisk on your left and a stile with a N.T. stone for 'Ulwell and Old Harry Rocks' on your right.

There is a water tank hidden beneath the overlying grassy mound and it holds a stone block labelled ' Swanage Water Act 1883. 489 ft above sea level'.

The obelisk was made from granite taken from near the Mansion House, London and was erected in 1892 - 'to commemorate the introduction of water from the chalk foundation into Swanage'. Fresh, clear, chalk-filtered water. A gallon or two of that would be quite welcome at the moment, wouldn't it?

However, this isn't the high point of Ballard Down. That honour goes to a point just 350 yards to the East so, to achieve your second peak today, follow the track up and along the ridge in the Old Harry Rocks direction. When you can't get any higher, that's it so turn round and come back to the obelisk.

Climb over the stile onto a clear, descending path alongside the RH wire fence. You'll soon be back at the lay-by. The path zig-zags its way down through gorse, past the waterworks enclosure in the valley on your left and past a group of scots pines. The clear downs over the RH fence are designated a Site of Special Scientific Interest (S.S.S.I). Anyway, the path creeps away from the fence near the bottom and steeply drops through a gorse path just before it joins the lower path which comes from the road crossing. At the junction, there is another sign-stone for 'Obelisk and Coast Path'.

Turn left and follow the path behind Wessex Water's fenced enclosure on your right, between trees and bushes until you emerge in a low paddock (frequently muddy). Climb over the gate or the kissing gate into the lay-by where you started. The kissing gate is substantial but too narrow to admit anybody wider than Twiggy - unless it's been changed.

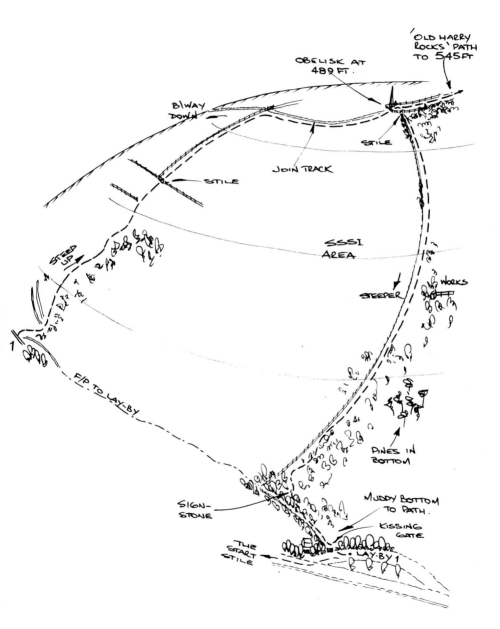

O.S. MAP NO. 193   REFERENCE SY 407922

Golden Cap is the highest peak on the Dorset Coast Path   For access, turn South off the A35 Bridport to Lyme Regis/Honiton road at Chideock into Duck Street - signposted for Seatown.   Bear right at the first fork into Seahill Lane and keep going until you find the Car Park - the starting point for this exploration.   You can go straight up to the top if you wish and quite rightly claim its ascent but the longer way round is a lovely walk through farmland and woods, through a deserted fishing village and past a ruined church - culminating in a fine ascent from the West side of Golden Cap.   This is the preferred route.

STAGE 1 - SEATOWN TO FILCOMBE WOOD   Leave the Car Park by crossing the footbridge over the River Winniford and walking down the road towards the sea.   (Ignore The Anchor Inn for now.   It'll still be there when you get back.) Turn up the Coast Path, signed 'Golden Cap 1 - Charmouth 3' and begin a slow climb, with some steps, over previously land-slipped ground.

Already, you can see along the coast to Lyme Regis, Beer and Devon until you bear right and go up more steps onto a high path with the cliff edge on your left and a fenced field on your right.   Keep to the steeply ascending path through brambles and sloes and, when you reach a fork in the path, take the right fork, signed 'Langdon Hill - Chideock', unless you are only here to add Golden Cap to your list.   In which case, bear left and follow the map only.   Return with Stage 1 below.

For the whole circuit, keep on up the grassy path and go over the stile into a long, rising field with a RH fence.   At the top, go over another stile onto a sloping gravel track with Langdon Hill wood facing you and turn left.   Follow the rising track with the LH hedge and the RH banked pine wood until you reach a RH barrier onto a woodland trail and a farm gate facing you.   Go through the Bridleway-arrowed gate and bear right up to the gate in the top RH corner of this rising field.   (The top LH corner gate leads straight up to Golden Cap).   On arrival at the gate, you will find a signpost for two Bridleways and one Footpath - signed 'Morecombelake'.   This is yours and it returns you somewhat by sending you down to a gate in the lower RH hedge.   I know you could have cut across the corner of the field - but that isn't the Footpath.   Go over the stile next to the gate (now with a Bridleway arrow) and follow the grass track between a banked RH fence and a low LH wood.   Now turn to Stage 2.

STAGE 1 - RETURN FROM GOLDEN CAP   Arriving at the top of Golden Cap (named from its gold coloured sand and its gorse flowers), go past the sign-stone for 'Seatown 1' and turn right, past three mounds to the edge of the cliff that overlooks the slumped lower landscape and the sea.   Take care!   After admiring the superb view, go back to the path and follow it past the Earl of Antrim's dedication stone to the O.S. trig point.   From here, follow the steep, stepped chalk path down through the gorse and bracken to the signposted gate at the bottom.   Go through and turn sharp right for 'Seatown', following the RH hedge down to a pair of stiles and some steps through a steep hedge.   The cliff edge is only just to your right but the path soon meanders away from it as it follows an old field edge of banked hawthorns on your left.   Keep straight on across a 300 yards long field, past a boggy area of marsh grass and a distant pair of wind-blown bushes.   Go over the stile in the far side hedge and follow the path down to meet the path which brought you up from Seatown. Just amble back now.   Hasn't it been a super walk - especially on the preferred route?

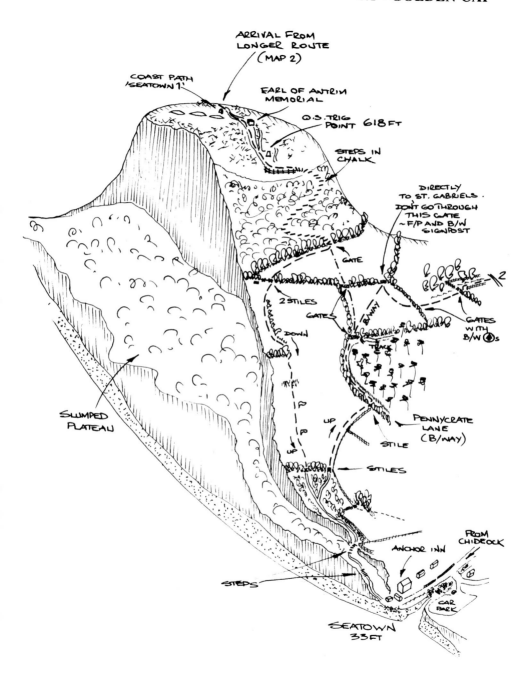

STAGE 2 - FILCOMBE WOOD TO GOLDEN CAP

Follow the grass track to another gate and stile (now with both Bridleway and Footpath arrows). Go over into a short, narrow green field with a banked hedge on your right and with another Bridleway-arrowed gate ahead. Over this next gate, you are in a farm area with concrete standing over to your left. Go straight on to yet another gate and stile with Bridleway and Footpath arrows. Over this stile, go past a brick and flint barn with steps and then walk quietly past Filcombe Farm cottage.

Immediately after the garden hedge, turn left through the field gate, signposted for 'St Gabriels 1/2 - Charmouth 3'. Go down the LH edge of this high-hedged and ash-bordered field into a sunken gateway in the bottom LH corner. Follow the LH edge of this next descending field to its end where a track runs along the bottom hedge to the right. Go over the stile, signposted 'St Gabriels' and join the track straight on through Gabriel's Wood. (Ignore the right fork track). When the track bends right, follow it round past the barrier in the LH corner. With a steep LH bank, the track narrows and then arrives at a stile and gate into a low, boggy field with marsh grass and running water over on your right.

Keep to the LH, fenced edge of the field where the path isn't at all distinct. Have faith though and you'll reach a footbridge over a stream which runs out of the LH wood. A signpost confirms that this is the way for 'St Gabriel's' so keep straight on, through another gate and onto a grassy path with a LH fence and hedge and a drop on your right down to the wooded stream.

Go through the next gate onto an even wider grassy plateau and keep following it along the top edge of a narrow field until you reach one more gate and stile. Go over, past the 'Langdon Hill and Morecombelake' signpost onto a concrete track which, the opposite signpost indicates, comes from 'Chardown Hill and Stonebarrow'.

Turn left and walk up to the open, track-filled area of the old fishing village of Stanton St Gabriel. I don't know what happened to the 'Stanton' bit. It seems to be disappearing from maps and everything. The row of brick and stone cottages are now rented out for holiday-lets by the National Trust. Bear left and follow the gravel track up between the LH hedge and the RH old walled orchard. Go through the top gate and follow the ascending grass and flint track around the ancient ruins of St Gabriel's church. A convenient, if not very comfortable, bench up on the bank affords pleasant views and a short rest.

Go through the next gate where the track keeps straight on up and around the LH hedged edge of the field. Don't follow it! Bear right as directed by the wooden 'Footpath' finger post and climb diagonally up this wide, long, steep field - aiming at a distant wooden post which will turn out to be another Coast Path signpost standing next to an N.T. barrier.

As you traverse the field, there are fine views along the coast to Lyme Regis and into Devon and I'm sure you won't need much coaxing to stop and look. Go through the barrier onto the winding chalk path and steps on the steep climb up the Western flank of Golden Cap. It's just as steep as Scarth Gap Pass en route for Haystacks in the Western Lakes but it's a lot shorter and Scarth Gap doesn't have a rope fence to pull yourself up on. Sorry. I mean 'on which to pull yourself up'.

At the top, turn to Stage 1 again. Congratulations on taking the scenic route.

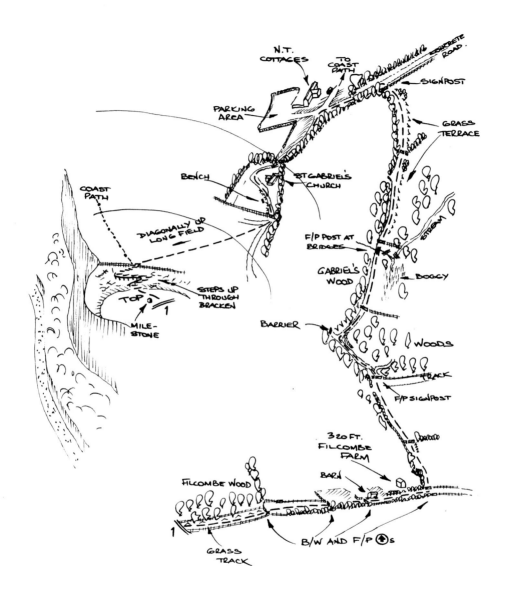

VIEWS AND INFORMATION

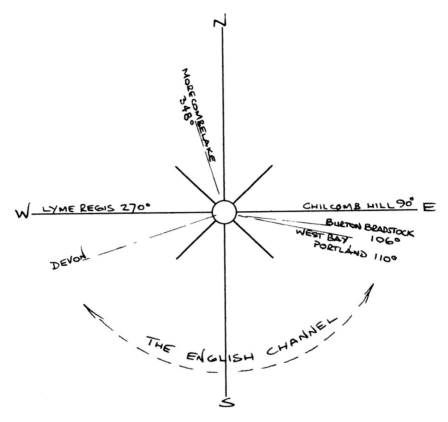

SEATOWN:
Ralph Wightman in 'Portrait of Dorset' sums up this lovely spot thus: "The handful of houses on this road carry the rather grand name of Seatown, but there is happily nothing resembling a town". It sits snugly between opposing steep cliffs of Golden Cap and Doghouse Hill.

STANTON ST GABRIEL:
This 'lost village' once supported 23 families - mostly of fishermen - and its little 13thC stone-built chapel was dedicated to St Gabriel. It was a chapel of ease to Whitchurch Canonicorum but, when a new chapel was built at Morecombelake on the Great Western Turnpike, it fell into disuse. The new chapel was dedicated on 2nd October 1841. Hutchins reported that the old hamlet of Stanton St Gabriel was "distant by 2 miles from Whitchurch or any other church and the way, joining to the sea, exposed to all violence of wind and weather, so that they can seldom repair to any church in winter". Fortunately, I cannot personally testify to the harshness of the environment as I have kept my visits to high summer.

INFORMATION AND VIEWS

CHILD OKEFORD:

Although Hutchins suggested that the name came from its 'chill' situation, the village always seems to be sheltered from the chill winds by Hambledon Hill on its Eastern flank.   However, the 'Okeford' part is probably true in referring to ancient oaks which stood near a ford on the Stour.   St Nicholas' Church was largely rebuilt by the Victorians but it retained its fine 15thC tower and a Norman font.

HAMBLEDON HILL:

Although Neolithic people settled on Hambledon Hill over 5000years ago and it has braved assaults from all sorts of invaders since then, it featured quite heavily in the Civil War as well.   In August 1645, several Royalist leaders were seized during a secret meeting in Shaftesbury.   Two days later the Dorset Clubmen ,who had mustered between 2500 and 4000 men, met up on Hambledon Hill to march on Shaftesbury to rescue the Royalists.   However, Cromwell was already on his way to Shaftesbury with 1000 dragoons.   After an hour-long battle, 60 Clubmen had been killed, 400 had been taken prisoner (including 4 rectors and curates) and 200 had been wounded. Of Cromwell's soldiers, 13 were killed.

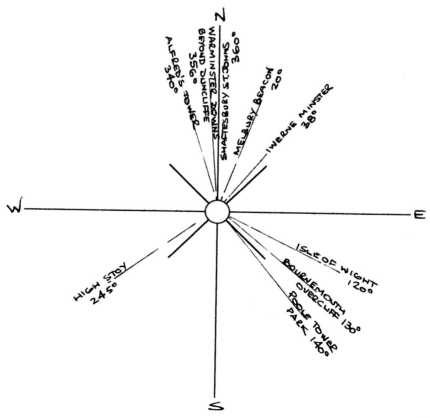

O.S. MAP NO. 194   REFERENCE ST 848123

Hambledon Hill is a National Nature Reserve covering 74 hectares and it once towered above the ancient forests which were cleared when Neolithic people settled here over 5000 years ago.   The starting point to the South West of the Hill is reached either from the A357 Blandford to Sturminster Newton road or the A350 Blandford to Shaftesbury road.   A small lay-by lies close to the starting Bridleway which can also be reached along a Footpath from Child Okeford.   If you begin in the churchyard of St Nicholas' in the village, you get tantalising glimpses of the bulk of Hambledon Hill towering above you before you begin the ascent, adding to the anticipation.

FROM CHILD OKEFORD - Cross the churchyard in a South-South-Easterly direction to the boundary wall which holds stepping stones and Footpath arrows. Over the wall, keep to the same direction across a long, narrowing field with a wood-fenced garden on your right and a fence on your left.   Follow the wooden fence around to your right, passing Footpath arrows, and then bear over to the left to another stile in the opposite fence.   In the next field, follow the RH hedge to one more stile in the far RH corner.   Another Footpath arrow points you past an old tree which lies in the bottom of a dip in this next long field.   Follow the RH hedge all the way to the far end of the field and go over the Footpath-signed stile in the corner onto a junction with the road and a left-turning track, signed 'Public Bridleway'.

FROM THE LAY-BY - Walk along the road towards Child Okeford and turn first right onto the rising track, signed 'Public Bridleway'.

EVERYBODY - Follow the rising grass and stone track past Markstone Cottages and up to a sharp right bend.   The sunken grass track which runs uphill beyond the gate is your return so make a mental note of it before going on up the track/hollow-way.   The track slowly ascends, bending left with trees on your right and a high bank on your left.   Go through a gate with a Bridleway arrow onto a grassy plateau - still climbing.   Levelling for a short distance, the iron age embankments of Hambledon Hill suddenly loom up on your left and, through another gate, the track is entrained between fences with the sweeping arena of Terrace Coppice over to your right.

When you emerge onto the open upper slopes, choose the steepest direction, bearing away from the LH fence (due East), and you will soon see a gate up ahead of you.   Go through the gate and walk over to the O.S. trig point for the highest point of this chalk ridge and the most expansive views.   The Wessex Ridgeway heads off over the other side but turn left down the fence-enclosed path to the Bridleway-arrowed gate.

Past the National Reserve notice, follow the path past high earthworks on your left and lower protuberances on your right.   Ignore the Bridleway which runs away to the right and ignore the grass tracks which run up through the earthworks on your left. Bear slightly left, ascending across about 100 yards of open grass to the highest point or peak of Hambledon Hill.   From here, the vast enclosure spreads away to your right and you could spend many hours up here exploring.   However, I've got to get you back down - so here goes.   Drop down the steep side of this high spot to the top of the first defensive ring and turn left.   Follow it, ascending slightly, to the first gap where there is a grassy track coming out of the hill-fort and running down the field to your right.   This is the sunken grass track which you saw through the gate earlier.   Just follow it back down and you'll soon be back at the start.

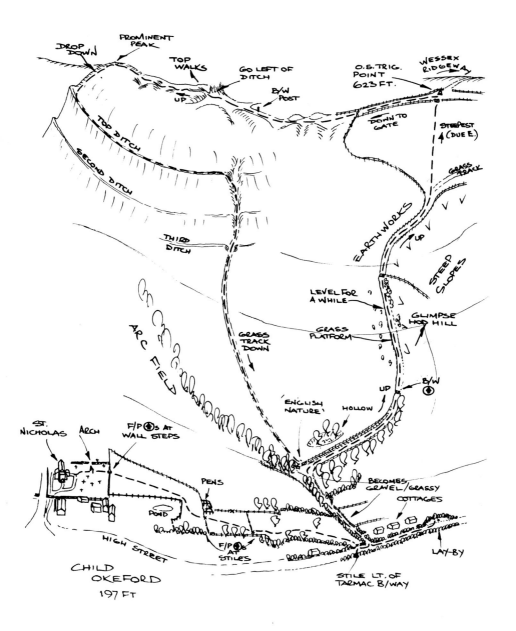

DROP DOWN

PROMINENT PEAK

TOP WALKS

GO LEFT OF DITCH

B/W POST

UP

O.S. TRIG. POINT 623 FT.

WESSEX RIDGEWAY

DOWN TO GATE

STEEPEST (DUE E.)

GRASS TRACK

TOP DITCH

SECOND DITCH

THIRD DITCH

EARTHWORKS

STEEP SLOPES

UP

LEVEL FOR A WHILE

GRASS PLATFORM

GLIMPSE HOD HILL

ARC FIELD

GRASS TRACK DOWN

ENGLISH NATURE

HOLLOW

UP

B/W

ST. NICHOLAS

ARCH

F/P ⦿s AT WALL STEPS

PENS

POND

BECOMES GRAVEL/GRASSY

COTTAGES

HIGH STREET

F/P ⦿ AT STILES

LAY-BY

CHILD OKEFORD 197 FT

STILE LT. OF TARMAC B/WAY

O.S. MAP NO. 193   REFERENCE SY 371988

You'll find Wootton Fitzpaine just 2 miles North of Charmouth off the A35 Bridport to Honiton road.   Follow the signs for the Parish Church for the starting point. This is a wonderful walk and the downs of Lambert's Castle Hill offer beautiful views over the Marshwood Vale and to the coast.   The approach is none too strenuous and the elevations are quite friendly for most of the way.

OUTWARD JOURNEY - STAGE 1

From the wide-verged approaches to the Parish Church, turn up the Footpath-arrowed track opposite the Church gates.   Past the RH house, keep left when a RH fork Footpath goes through a gate.   Follow the sunken, grassy track to an unsigned gate and go through onto a rising field.   A faint grass track comes through the next LH gate, arrowed for Liberty Trail and the Wessex Ridgeway.   Follow the rising grass path across to the top gate - about 100 yards up from the bottom LH corner.

At this gate, more L/Tr and W/R arrows point up the next field.   Now, stay just below the ridge but don't venture down the LH slope.   On the way, adjust your line for a holly bush in the far corner where the hedge meets a wire fence.   Go over the stile in the corner into a big field which slopes down to the left.   Walk along the level ledge for a few yards and then bear left slightly, aiming for a distant stile in the wire fence which borders the farm track on the other side of your field.   Above your RH ridge, there is a gate in the hedge onto the road.   Have a quick look over the ridge at it because this is where you come back and it will help to know where it comes in again.   Now, having found the stile with a Bridleway arrow this side and a Footpath arrow the other side, go over onto the track and turn left down the hill with a ditch and hedge on your right.

Follow the track down past a turn to Great Coombe Farmhouse and, close to the RH hedges and banks, past the barns and cowsheds.   Close all of the gates after you and keep straight on up a wide hedged track with a ditch changing sides en route.   Ignore the LH Footpath past a steel barn and follow the track up, round a left bend and onto the concreted corner of a track which turns down to another farmyard on your left.   A private path goes up into Coney's Castle woods on your right.   Now turn to Stage 2.

RETURNING FROM STAGE 2

The track degenerates into sheep paths but, through the next gate, it becomes a grass track again.   Past a set of three stunted oaks and a row of oaks on your right, bear slightly left to go past a stone barn and through a farm gate onto a short track which passes to the left of a cottage with a good garden.   Don't follow their track down to the left but go straight on through the half-gate into a rising field, still with Coney's Castle woods up on your right.   Follow the old grass track near the LH hedge all the way to a gate at the end where you emerge onto the road from Coney's Castle by a Bridleway arrow post.   Turn left down the road and past the track for Great Coombe Farm which you joined further down earlier today.   Go through the next gate with the plethora of arrows on your right, bear left across the field and head back to the holly bush and the stile which you came over on your way to Lambert's Castle Hill.

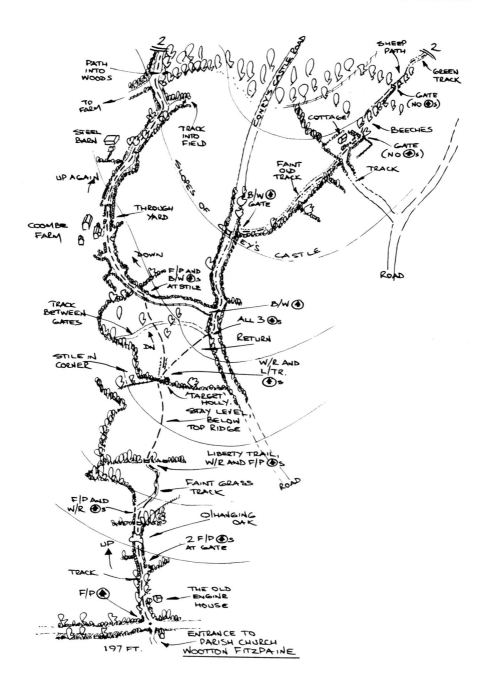

PATH INTO WOODS

TO FARM

STEEL BARN

UP AGAIN

COOMBE FARM

THROUGH YARD

DOWN

TRACK INTO FIELD

SLOPES OF

F/P AND B/W ⊕s AT STILE

TRACK BETWEEN GATES

STILE IN CORNER

DN

CONEY'S CASTLE ROAD

SHEEP PATH

GREEN TRACK

GATE (NO ⊕s)

COTTAGE

BEECHES

GATE (NO ⊕s)

TRACK

FAINT OLD TRACK

B/W ⊕ GATE

...EY'S CASTLE

ROAD

B/W ⊕

ALL 3 ⊕s

RETURN

W/R AND L/TR. ⊕s

'TARGET' HOLLY. STAY LEVEL BELOW TOP RIDGE

LIBERTY TRAIL, W/R AND F/P ⊕s

ROAD

FAINT GRASS TRACK

F/P AND W/R ⊕s

O'HANGING OAK

2 F/P ⊕s AT GATE

UP

TRACK

F/P ⊕

THE OLD ENGINE HOUSE

ENTRANCE TO PARISH CHURCH WOOTTON FITZPAINE

197 FT.

STAGE 2 - TO LAMBERT'S CASTLE AND BACK

OUTWARD -

Still rising steeply along the grass and gravel track with heather and gorse on the RH bank, there is a large plantation of new trees behind the line of older ones on the RH side. At the top of the rise, there are gates into fields on both sides of the track and a good view across the head of the Fishpond Bottom valley on your left. Follow the more level track with a RH verge to a gate and out onto a junction of five roads. The road immediately to your right as you emerge from the track is the one which bisects Coney's Castle. The best - and safest - way to enjoy Coney's Castle is to circumnavigate it as we are doing. You approached this spot by keeping to the West of the hill and you will return by the East.

Keep straight on past the three-way pointer on the LH corner and across the grass triangle with a sign for 'Marshwood'. In front of you is a rising, stony path with the National Trust sign for 'Lambert's Castle Hill'. Go past the Liberty Trail, Wessex Ridgeway and Footpath arrows and, with gorse and birch either side, climb up to a gate with a 'Keep Dogs Under Control' notice. Go through onto the steeply rising, flint and grass path and keep on up until you emerge onto the wide ridge of the hill with wide grass areas running along the top between banks of heather and birch trees.

You can wander at will over the hill but the best views are reserved for the route along the West side (the RH side). The West side drops away more steeply whilst the East is more gradual and allows the trees to mask the view. If you stay on the RH side for a while, you'll find a couple of benches but, to find the O.S. trig point, walk to the end of the line of birches on your left. Go right around the end, doubling back a little to the far side of a large clump of trees on the other side of the second grass route. When you've found it - and found that you can't see anything but grass and trees from here, keep heading in your original direction and you'll find a cross dyke and the hilltop plateau.

RETURN JOURNEY -

Dragging yourself away, return to the five-ways junction and take the turning for 'Whitchurch' (That's Whitchurch Canonicorum). Go down the lane and past the cottage on the LH corner. Just past their garden, turn right through the gate with the Bridleway arrow into a long sloping field. The field slopes down to the lane hedge on the left whilst your old, levelled and grassy track follows the contours of Coney's Castle with gorse up on the steep RH slopes. You have beautiful views over the Marshwood Vale from here and, if you look back between Lambert's Castle and the first lower pylon, you will be able to make out St Mary's Church in Marshwood. This has to be the very best part of Coney's Castle hill. The road goes through the middle and there is a car park up on the top as well. It is crowned with trees though, so the views are much better from here.

Keep to the vague grass track and try not to disturb the sheep. Now, turn back to Stage 1 for the rest of the journey back.

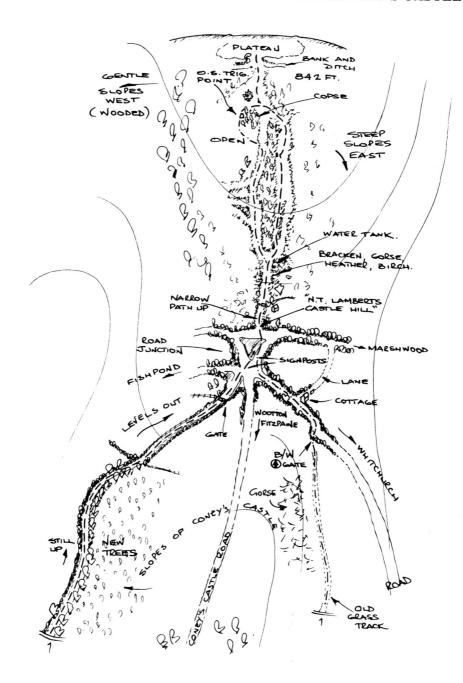

PLATEAU

BANK AND
DITCH
842 FT.

O.S. TRIG.
POINT

GENTLE
SLOPES
WEST
(WOODED)

COPSE

OPEN

STEEP
SLOPES
EAST

WATER TANK.

BRACKEN GORSE
HEATHER, BIRCH.

NARROW
PATH UP

"N.T. LAMBERTS
CASTLE HILL"

ROAD
JUNCTION

MARSHWOOD

SIGNPOSTS

FISH POND

LANE

COTTAGE

LEVELS OUT

WOOTTON
FITZPAINE

GATE

B/W
GATE

WHITCHURCH

GORSE
CASTLE

STILL
UP

NEW
TREES

SLOPES OF CONEY'S

CONEY'S CASTLE ROAD

ROAD

OLD
GRASS
TRACK

1

1

8 - LAMBERTS CASTLE

VIEWS AND INFORMATION

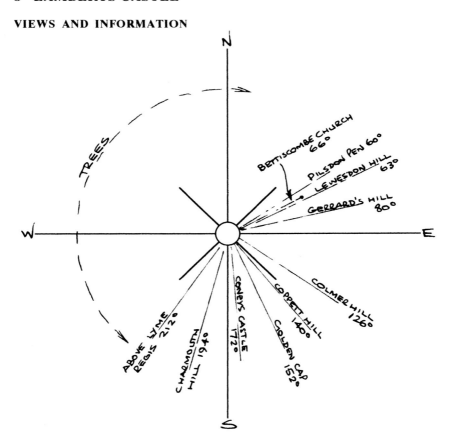

WOOTTON FITZPAINE:
Wodeton in the Domesday Book, held by Bretel of the Earl of Moreton.   The Parish Church is based on Norman foundations and has a 15thC tower and chapel.   The rest was largely rebuilt by the Victorians but it stands in a very pleasant spot and is well worth a visit on your return to Wootton Fitzpaine.

CONEY'S CASTLE:
Although rabbits abound on these slopes, the hill doesn't get its name from coneys but from a Danish chieftain named Conig.   The hill has seen many a battle between the Saxons and the Danes. . On its Western side, the hill drops into Fishpond Bottom (where your path ascends) where a tiny stream runs down to join the River Char.

LAMBERT'S CASTLE:
I couldn't wax more lyrical about this beautiful Dorset height than did Monica Hutchings who said, "From the open hill top with its many picnic places, its beech plantations and stretches of deep crimson heath and heather, the sea can be glimpsed through breaks in the rim of the vale (Marshwood) to Southward.

INFORMATION AND VIEWS

COMPTON ABBAS:
Compton, meaning 'farm in the valley', comes from 'cumb' and 'tun'. In 955 AD a Charter granted 10 hides of land in Compton to the Nunnery of Shaftesbury - hence the 'Abbas' connection. The first church, in East Compton, was pulled down and some of the stones were used in the foundation of the 1866 Church of St Mary. Many of the old church's fitting were also transferred including its Norman font, five bells and a 1665 plain silver chalice.

EAST COMPTON:
Only the late 15thC West tower and West wall of the former nave still stand, albeit defiantly, in its consecrated grounds with several remaining small monuments and gravestones. The Manor Farm house is late 18thC. As you will see, there is a clear cross-dyke running across Melbury Hill, about 300 yards long, and running all the way into Melbury Abbas parish.

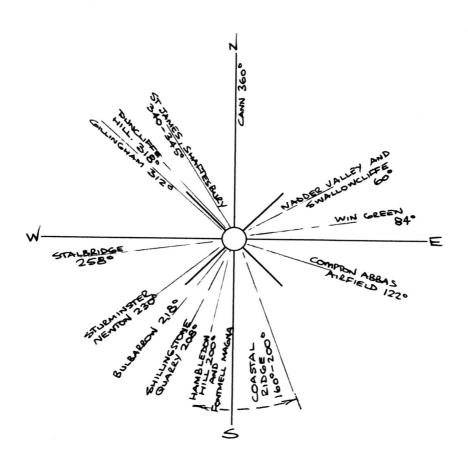

O.S. MAP NO. 183   REFERENCE ST 873198

Melbury Beacon stands proudly on the Western boundary escarpment of Cranborne Chase hovering precipitously above the Stour Valley and the Blackmore Vale. Although the third highest peak in this book of walks, the height gained on this climb is only just over 500 ft because the nearest suitable starting point at Compton Abbas is already 352 ft above sea level.   Compton Abbas stands on the A350, about 3 miles South of Shaftesbury and limited parking is available by St Mary's Church near the bus stop for the Wilts and Dorset X13, X38 and 139 or Rural Bus 47.

The name of Compton comes from 'cumb' and 'tun' meaning 'farm in the valley'.   In 955 AD, a Charter granted 10 hides of land in Compton to the Nunnery at Shaftesbury - hence the 'Abbas' connection.   The first church, of indeterminate date, was pulled down and some of the stones were used in the foundations of this 1866 Church of St Mary.   It has a Norman font and a chalice of 1665 - the "Cumpton Abbies Cup".

Begin the walk by passing through the school grounds and out into the lane opposite The Old Forge (B & B at the time of writing).   Turn right at the foot of the steps and take the level lane (not the right-descending lane).   Follow the lane, past another right turn, past Lots Cottage and a row of cottages on the right and past a Footpath through a farm gate on your left.   After a Bridleway on your right, you arrive at the original St Mary's church whose glaucanitic sandstone tower still stands aloof in its small graveyard.

After the walled farmyard on your left and the RH turning to Gourds Farm on your right, turn right onto a Bridleway-signed track.   Go through the gate and follow the LH fence up to another gate facing you.   Go through this gate as well and cross this next field diagonally left towards the top LH corner where you will find another gate. Through here, you will find a National Trust sign for 'Melbury Down'.

Follow the chalk track as it climbs the lower slopes of Melbury Hill but, as it bends right to run alongside the top fence - aiming for a farm gate - turn left and walk straight up to a wicket gate where you will find a Bridleway arrow and a N.T. Footpath arrow.   Go through the gate and turn left to follow the wire fence on varying degrees of incline all the way to the top of the hill.   Here, climb over the stile to find the O.S. trig point at 865 ft.

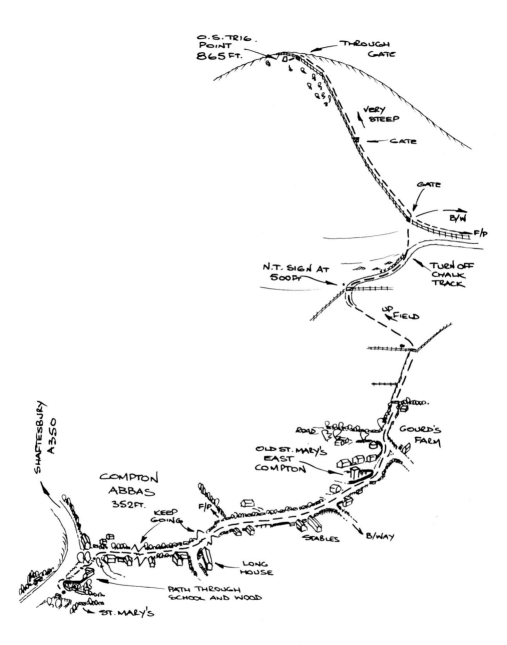

O.S. MAP NO. 194   REFERENCE ST 819093/801084

Approach Okeford Fitzpaine from Shillingstone on the A357 Blandford/Sturminster Newton road.   Wilts and Dorset buses 190, 237, 303 and 312 attend Okeford Fitzpaine as does local bus 40.

It's only a short climb to the top of Okeford Hill so I have added an excursion to Bell Hill as well.   Not only does this afford spectacular views over the Blackmore Vale but I have been able to introduce a little Lakeland reality to the journey.   When climbing Scafell Pike, the summit comes into view eventually but, just as elation is about to strike, you suddenly realise that there is a steep descent from Broad Crag and an ascent of an extra 300ft before you can actually touch the summit cairn.   After such a long climb, it's quite a blow and, in a similar yet easier way, this walk includes a descent of 273ft from the top of Okeford Hill down into Turnworth Woods and a steady uphill stroll of 349ft to the heights of Bell Hill.   However, the stupendous views and the visit to the deserted settlement of Ringmoor make such suffering well worthwhile.

STAGE 1 - OKEFORD FITZPAINE TO OKEFORD HILL AND THE TURNWORTH ROAD

This walk starts in Back Lane on the far side of St Andrew's Church in the village. Walk up the lane to its T-junction with a track/Bridleway and turn left.   Follow the track around and through a gate onto Okeford Hill, passing an old quarry on your right.   After the fence-enclosed grass-topped water tank, follow the path to the gate which opens onto the hill road.   Take note of this gate as this is the gate which you'll need when you're coming back.   For now, turn away from the road and go through the gate into the next, higher field.   Aim diagonally up to the next gate and, through this, follow the same line to yet another gate.   Keep to the same line, with the Armada beacon up on your right.

Becoming closer to the top fence, go through the gate and cross the forest track into the facing wood.   Follow the well-used, wide track to its first cross-track junction. Turn right and walk up to another junction of tracks.   Cross straight over, bearing slightly right to follow the path along the RH edge of the wide field with the woods on your right.   At the far end, where the path turns right to follow the edge of the woods, go through the personnel gate onto a track along the top edge of a large, descending field and turn left.   If you don't want to visit Ringmoor or the heights of Bell Hill, you could turn right here and get back to the road for the return to Okeford Fitzpaine.

Follow the top edge of the field to a junction with a LH track and a gate into Bonsley Woods.   Don't go through the gate but turn right and follow the edge of the high-hedged field down the ever-steepening field.   Go through the gate in the bottom corner and bear right to follow the edge of a steeply dropping wood, dropping down this steep field to a gate onto the road at the bottom.

Through the gate, cross over the road into the parking area opposite.   Go through the gate into the Footpath-arrowed and National Trust-signed parkland.   Go between the left two of three oaks and walk up the steep hill and under an overhanging oak.

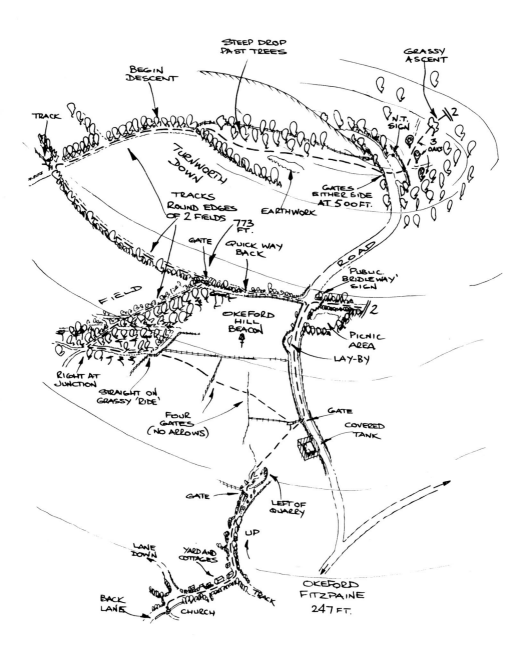

STEEP DROP PAST TREES

GRASSY ASCENT

BEGIN DESCENT

TRACK

N.T. SIGN

TURNWORTH DOWN

3 OAKS

GATES EITHER SIDE AT 500 FT.

EARTHWORK

TRACKS ROUND EDGES OF 2 FIELDS

773 FT.

GATE

QUICK WAY BACK

ROAD

PUBLIC BRIDLEWAY SIGN

FIELD

OKEFORD HILL BEACON

PICNIC AREA

LAY-BY

RIGHT AT JUNCTION

STRAIGHT ON GRASSY 'RIDE'

FOUR GATES (NO ARROWS)

GATE

COVERED TANK

GATE

LEFT OF QUARRY

UP

LANE DOWN

YARD AND COTTAGES

OKEFORD FITZPAINE 247 FT.

BACK LANE

CHURCH

TRACK

STAGE 2 - TURNWORTH ROAD TO BELL HILL AND BACK TO OKEFORD FITZPAINE

The path bears right onto a very wide grassy ride which soon reduces to a normal width track through woodland and coppice. Still rising, the grassy track goes through a more open area with ridges crossing your route. Through two gates with no arrows, go up a very long field with ridges and bumps everywhere. These are the earthworks which you could see from the top of Bonsley Common before you began your descent to the Turnworth road. They are all that remain of the ancient settlement of Ringmoor.

Keep climbing slowly but taking the time to wonder about the fate of this settlement and to enjoy the gentle stroll. After a group of ridges on your left, before the fenced oaks, the route goes up and over a steep ridge which crosses the whole width of the field. From here, you can see the top Blandford to Shaftesbury road and the edge of Cranborne Chase over to your right. The path now passes two ash trees standing in a hole on your left and, after another pair of very clear ridges come across the field, there is another tree-filled hole on your right.

After a ruined brick and flint barn behind the LH fence, bear slightly right towards the gates in the top RH corner. Go through the unmarked smaller gate and past a singularly uninviting pond in its enclosure of fences and hedges. As the field compresses into a narrow space, go through the gate by a National Trust sign for 'Ringmoor and Turnworth' and turn right. Just a minute though. To truly 'bag' Bell Hill, you will have to turn left first and follow the fence and hedge-enclosed track for 350 yards until you reach a couple of gates and a private stile in the RH fence. This is the highest spot on Bell Hill (except maybe the tumulus in the field beyond the stile - but that's private land).

So, sit on the stile and look round at the lovely views of the Blackmore Vale and - on a clear day - the Welsh mountains. Honest! You are now at a height of 773 ft.

Returning to the N.T. sign by the pond, follow the track past confirmation Bridleway and Wessex Ridgeway arrows. This track descends slightly and provides lovely open views towards your ridge-top walk earlier today. As you approach a LH bend past a pair of gates on your left, you can actually look down on Hambledon Hill ahead of you. There are superb views to Stalbridge, Marnhull and all places between.

After a pair of barns, one either side of the track, the track keeps descending and becomes somewhat sunken between hedges until you reach the Okeford Hill Car Park/Picnic Area on your left. The track runs out here and crosses the road to continue back towards Bonsley Woods. Those who cut short this walk will have come back to this crossing along that track.

Now, turn left and walk carefully along the road past the picnic area and the lay-by opposite. Continue down the road towards Okeford Fitzpaine and think where you found the gate on the way up - as your path came to the road and then turned away again. It isn't the first gate you find on your right. It's the next one - about 200 yards after it. If you reach the grassed-over water tank, you've gone too far.

Having found the gate (un-signed), go through and retrace your first steps down into Okeford Fitzpaine at the end of a lovely walk and having conquered another pair of Dorset's peaks.

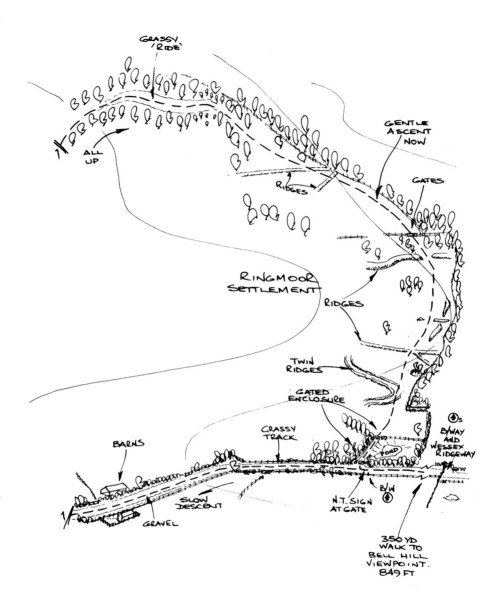

GRASSY 'RIDE'

ALL UP

GENTLE ASCENT NOW

GATES

RIDGES

RINGMOOR SETTLEMENT

RIDGES

TWIN RIDGES

GATED ENCLOSURE

GRASSY TRACK

BARNS

POND

B/WAY AND WESSEX RIDGEWAY

S

B/W

SLOW DESCENT

GRAVEL

N.T. SIGN AT GATE

350 YD WALK TO BELL HILL VIEWPOINT. 849 FT

10 - OKEFORD HILL AND BELL HILL

INFORMATION AND VIEWS FROM BELL HILL

OKEFORD FITZPAINE:
In the Domesday Book as 'Adford held by the Church of St Mary, Glastonbury', Okeford Fitzpaine has previously been Ockford Alured (from the common Christian name of Alured amongst the ruling DeLincolnias) and Ockford Nichole (from the surname of a later, French, ruling lord).   It has been Fitzpaine since Edward I who granted Robert Fitzpaine a Charter to hold markets and fairs.   The Church of St Andrew was rebuilt completely in 1866 and it has a splendid triangular Victorian font. It stands on the site of an earlier 12thC edifice whilst a 14thC replacement was consecrated in 1302 and extended in Tudor times.

BONSLEY COMMON:
On the descent to the Turnworth road, the obvious scattered tumuli on the hill are remains of Bronze Age burial mounds.

RINGMOOR SETTLEMENT:
Climbing up from the same road, the array of ridges, hollows and tracks are all that remains of the Ringmoor settlement.   Sadly, more useful information is hard to find.

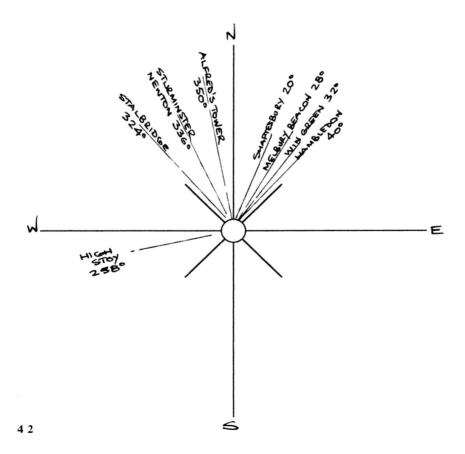

VIEWS AND INFORMATION

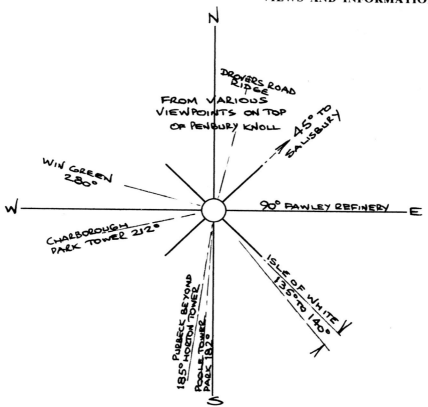

PENTRIDGE:
A most unusual dedication, this.   The Parish Church of Pentridge is dedicated to St Rumbold and the 14thC church was completely rebuilt in 1855 in the original style but sports a stone spire.   There is another Dorset literary connection here since a commemorative plaque was erected here in 1902 to Robert Browning, the poet.   The Browning family grave is in the little churchyard and another Robert Browning, who died in 1746, is amongst the occupiers.

PENBURY KNOLL:
The hill fort is pear shaped and covers an area of 3.3/4 acres inside its rings.   As it stands on a cap of Reading Beds over flint-filled clay, it was much damaged by shallow quarrying.   The Roman excavated the hilltop for the rounded pebbles which were so useful for building roads - especially the Ackling Dyke which runs just the other side of Pentridge.   This is the road from Old Sarum (Salisbury) which runs past Badbury Rings on its way to Maiden Castle (Dorchester).

O.S. MAP NO. 184   REFERENCE SU 040171

Pentridge lies 3/4 mile from the A354 Blandford to Salisbury road, barely 3 miles from Wiltshire and 1.1/2 miles from Hampshire.   The nearest buses are Wilts and Dorset 184 and 185 and local bus 400, all stopping on the A354.   Parking in the village is limited and should be kept to the main street.   This is a lovely walk, almost entirely upon Pentridge Hill's clear, breezy down with no long jaunt to get there.

Starting in the main street, walk towards the church at the South-West end but don't turn into the church turning at the cottage called Chestnuts.   After the walled garden of Pentridge House, go over the Footpath-arrowed stile in the garden fence of the next LH house with the staddle stones alongside their gravel drive.   Aim just past the first large tree towards the opposite tree-covered bank.   You will find another Footpath-arrowed stile which leads you into a sunken, rising chalky path lined with trees and bushes.   You will have glimpses of a tennis court and paddock on your left and an open field on your right as you ascend to another stile with a Footpath arrow.

Go over onto the slopes of Pentridge Hill with a wire fence on your right.   Follow the fence until it turns right with two Footpath arrows.   Follow the uphill angled arrow and take aim for the centre of the capping of pines trees on the hilltop.   This will lead you (at 154 degrees) through a gap between a line of gorse bushes on a grassy bank.   Still climbing steeply, either go around the LH end of a cloak of gorse bushes (at 144 degrees) or around the RH end (at 182 degrees).   Either way, you will soon find yourself walking over a defensive ring into the scattered pines.

The extensive earthworks are the remains of Penbury Knoll hill fort - together with later excavations when the rounded pebbles of the Reading Beds were quarried for road surfacing by the Romans.   Wander at will all over the hilltop and enjoy the high earthworks and the pines.   Enjoy the views as well - not only on this side but from the fence which borders the valley of Toby's Bottom on the South-West.   You will find the O.S. trig point on a small, scrub-protected knoll at the East end of the woods.

The return journey begins with a descent from the knoll, above a depression with an uninviting pool at the bottom.   At first, the route keeps quite close to the top fence, undulating and meandering, with some superb views to the East and South-East but then begins a gradual descent on a vague green track along open ground with a few scattered bushes dotted about.   The best guide I can offer is to keep just below the descending ridge whilst keeping the natural amphitheatre in view on your left.   If you can't see it, you've gone too far right.   Soon, you will pass some complicated earthworks on top of the ridge and then, with the track becoming definitely more clear, you pass a series of chalk and flint pits on your right.   Just after another pit on your left (with trees in), the track becomes deeper and grassy.

Within a few yards, you meet a sunken track coming down from your right, near a horse-jump and a Jubilee Trail-arrowed stile in the facing wire fence.   Turn left, downhill, towards a gate in the corner of joining wire fenced fields.   Go through onto a short, descending, fence-enclosed track to 1.1/2 gates.   These lead onto the chalk track which runs past Whitey Top Dairy Farm.   Past the milking parlour, keep to the hedge-bordered and sunken track all the way to the T-junction at the foot of the hill.   Turn left and follow the bank and verge-edged track back along the valley floor, past the lane from the A354 to where you started.   What a gorgeous walk!

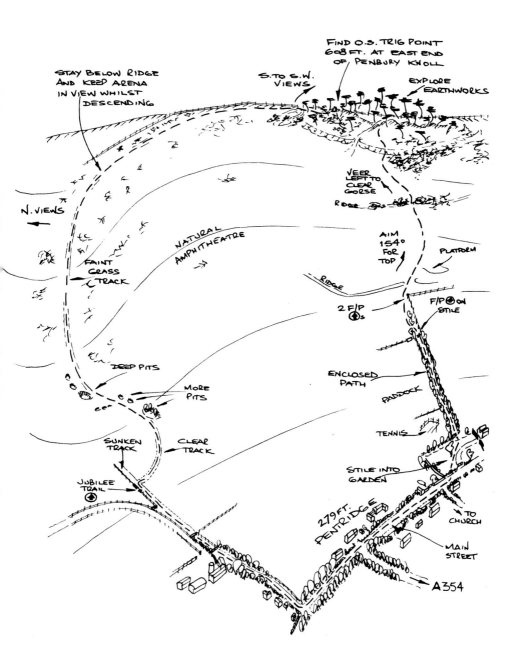

FIND O.S. TRIG POINT
608 FT. AT EAST END
OF PENBURY KNOLL

STAY BELOW RIDGE
AND KEEP ARENA
IN VIEW WHILST
DESCENDING

S. TO S.W.
VIEWS

EXPLORE
EARTHWORKS

N. VIEWS

VEER
LEFT TO
CLEAR
GORSE

RIDGE

NATURAL
AMPHITHEATRE

AIM
154°
FOR
TOP

PLATFORM

FAINT
GRASS
TRACK

RIDGE

2 F/P
S

F/P ON
STILE

ENCLOSED
PATH

PADDOCK

DEEP PITS

MORE
PITS

TENNIS

SUNKEN
TRACK

CLEAR
TRACK

STILE INTO
GARDEN

JUBILEE
TRAIL

279 FT.
PENTRIDGE

TO
CHURCH

MAIN
STREET

A354

12 - PILSDON PEN AND LEWESDON HILL   908 FT/895 FT

O.S. MAP NO. 193   REFERENCE ST 413012/437011

Approaching Broadwindsor from Beaminster on the B3163, you will find a one-way system in operation.   I found the widest place for parking with the least amount of traffic is outside the church railings just round the corner on the Mosterton road.

It's a very pleasant farmland walk followed by a final steep assault to get to the top of Pilsdon Pen but, as Broadwindsor is already 497 ft above sea level before you even start, I have added the walk and climb to Lewesdon Hill as well.   The overall height gain is then 651 ft which makes the excursion well worth while.   The superb views over the Marshwood Vale towards the coast from Pilsdon Pen are complemented by the farm walk and the bird song-filled woodland walk to the top of Lewesdon Hill.

STAGE 1 - BROADWINDSOR TO PILSDON PEN

This walk starts in the Mosterton road on the far side of the Parish Church of the Nativity of St John the Baptist.   Through the churchyard, cross over the B3162 and follow the opposite lane down and up again, past houses on either side, to the right turning for 'Hursey'.   Follow this lane between houses and cottages until the lane bends right at bend 'X' on your map.   There are two hollow-ways with a field gate in between but go through the last gate (with a Footpath arrow) into the rising field.

This is a steep field and, when you reach the top, keep following the banked hedge on your left down to the bottom corner.   Go through the gap in the hedge into a very long field with a huge ash tree half-way across on the slope.   Past the tree (due West) you will arrive at a half-gate into the churchyard of St Andrew's Church, Burstock. After visiting the old stone, mullioned windowed Manor Farm and the village, come back to this gate and head up the field to the right, turning into the near RH corner where you will find a stile with two Footpath-arrows.   Turn sharp left and walk up the steep field to the top fence, then turn right to another Footpath-arrowed stile near the top.   Go over the stile and bear right towards the LH end of the short hedge.   A sunken grassy track then leads you down to an un-arrowed gate onto a tarmac lane.

Cross over onto the concrete track leading to Burstock Grange Farm but turn instantly right into an open area with a big barn on your left.   Go through the gate into a hilltop field and aim for the RH end of Pilsdon Pen (due West).   When you can see it, go down to the opening in the opposite hedge.   Cross straight over a grassy track with a Bridleway gate on your left.   In this next field, bear slightly left.   Descend the field diagonally and you will find a double stile around the corner.   Over the stile, follow the hedge down to the RH corner.   Go over the Wessex Ridgeway-arrowed stile onto a fenced track and turn left to follow the track to its hedged end.   Turn left at the T-junction with W/R and Footpath arrows on the gateposts and follow the track round to a gate into the concrete yard of Lower Newnham Farm.   Go up the yard and turn right at the top.   When you reach the rising, fenced gravel track, turn left and head up the steep hill.   After a row of LH trees, both natural and ornamental, cross over the road to a gateway with a Public Footpath post and a W/R arrow.

Go through onto an even steeper, fenced gravel track, stopping to admire the fine views behind you as often as you like.   At the top, go through the gate onto the steeply sloping field which clads the slopes of Pilsdon Pen.   Bear right and aim for the top RH corner where the top hedge meets the rising fence on your right.

4 6

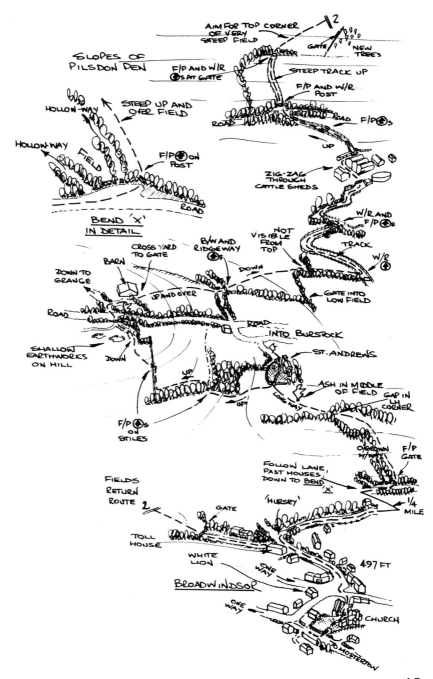

AIM FOR TOP CORNER OF VERY STEEP FIELD

2

GATE

NEW TREES

SLOPES OF PILSDON PEN

F/P AND W/R Os AT GATE

STEEP TRACK UP

F/P AND W/R POST

HOLLOW-WAY

STEEP UP AND OVER FIELD

ROAD

ROAD   F/POs

HOLLOW-WAY

FIELD

F/POON POST

UP

ROAD

ZIG-ZAG THROUGH CATTLE SHEDS

BEND 'X' IN DETAIL

W/R AND F/POs

CROSS YARD TO GATE

B/W AND RIDGEWAY Os

DOWN

NOT VISIBLE FROM TOP

TRACK

W/R O

BARN

DOWN TO GRANGE

UP AND OVER

ROAD

GATE INTO LOW FIELD

SHALLOW EARTHWORKS ON HILL

DOWN

ROAD

INTO BURSTOCK

ST. ANDREWS

UP

UP

ASH IN MIDDLE OF FIELD   GAP IN LH CORNER

F/P Os ON STILES

O/GROWN H/WAY

F/P GATE

FOLLOW LANE, PAST HOUSES, DOWN TO BEND 'X'

FIELDS RETURN ROUTE

2

GATE

'HURSEY'

¼ MILE

TOLL HOUSE

WHITE LION

ONE WAY

497 FT

BROADWINDSOR

ONE WAY

CHURCH

TO MOSTERTON

STAGE 2 - PILSDON PEN TO LEWESDON HILL AND BACK TO BROADWINDSOR

At the top, the path bears right at Footpath and W/R arrows onto a narrow grassy shelf between the banks of Pilsdon Pen and the plantation of new trees on its slopes. Follow the path for a few yards and then turn left over an arrowed stile and a slide-stile onto the National Trust-signed path into Pilsdon Pen itself. When the RH fence turns to its right, the Wessex Ridgeway follows it around the lower rings but you can go straight through the openings in the banks of the enclosure. Stroll around the top rings and enjoy the fabulous views at will but make sure you end up at the O.S. trig point. Having feasted your eyes on the delights all around, take the stepped path down the South-East end to the National Trust sign and the stile onto the B3164.

Cross over to the small car park and turn left to follow the hedged, banked and tree-lined road for 1 mile. It's a very pleasant stroll with some good views. After the initial lane by the car park, down to Pilsdon hamlet, the only turnings along the road are - left to the Newnham Farms and Courtwood Farm and right to Swilletts Farm. When the road bends to the left at a small barn, a lane turns off right to Wall Farm. Turn into this lane but then go instantly left onto a climbing, deep hollow-way with overhanging beech trees. The track meanders ever upwards and affords good views to your left at intervals whilst the bank on your right rarely allows such luxuries.

Past a gate on the RH side, the track becomes quite narrow and plunges into bracken - still rising, dropping and meandering. There is a glimpse of Golden Cap and then the track becomes sunken in a deep, dark hollow-way again. However, forget the distant views. There are more to come. Instead, enjoy the closeness of these fine old beech trees, the rustling of the leaves and the bird song that you don't get in pine woods. When the wood expands to the right, keep following the bank-enclosed path and you will meet a few Bridleway arrows in a wood of younger beech trees.

Eventually, the track opens out in front with spaced old beeches in the LH bank and the wood spreading upward beyond the RH bank. The track is somewhat muddy along here but the woodland side is kinder to walkers. Keep straight on until you reach a National Trust 'Lewesdon Hill' sign and a rising gravel track on your right. Arrows confirm that this is a Footpath whilst the track which continues straight ahead without you is a Bridleway.

Climb up this steep track, becoming grassier near the top, and you suddenly reach a plateau with gorse and scrub growing in a framework of beeches and scots pines. You'll know when you've reached the end because the plateau drops on all of the other sides. Straight ahead, you can make out Golden Cap beyond a large scots pine. There isn't an O.S. trig point but the end point stands at 895 ft above sea level. When you've stayed long enough, turn back and go down the track to where you joined it from the Bridleway and cross straight over to a stile with a Footpath arrow.

Go over into a steeply descending field with a deep hollow down on your right, filled with a wood. Follow the LH bank of beeches down to a gate into the second of four fields on this descent. All of the gates carry Footpath labels and arrows and each is in a straight line with its predecessor. The last field is on something of a tapering ridge so you can't see the last gate. However, aim for the LH of the group of cottages and you'll soon see it. Go through it, down the gravel track and you'll come back out onto the road, before the Hursey turning, at 'Toll House'. Just stroll back up into Broadwindsor at the end of a tiring but wholly enjoyable day.

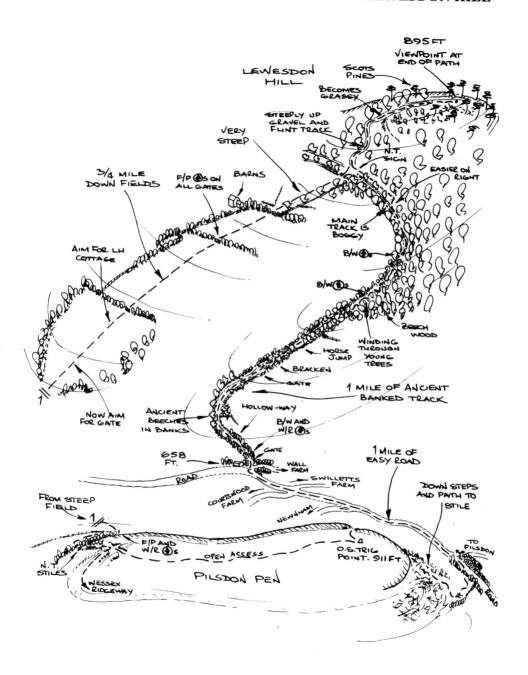

895 FT
VIEWPOINT AT END OF PATH

SCOTS PINES

BECOMES GRASSY

LEWESDON HILL

STEEPLY UP GRAVEL AND FLINT TRACK

VERY STEEP

N.T. SIGN

EASIER ON RIGHT

3/4 MILE DOWN FIELDS

F/P (s) ON ALL GATES

BARNS

MAIN TRACK IS BOGGY

B/W (s)

AIM FOR LH COTTAGE

B/W (s)

BEECH WOOD

WINDING THROUGH YOUNG TREES

HORSE JUMP

BRACKEN

GATE

1 MILE OF ANCIENT BANKED TRACK

HOLLOW-WAY

NOW AIM FOR GATE

ANCIENT BEECHES IN BANKS

B/W AND W/R (s)

658 FT.

GATE

1 MILE OF EASY ROAD

ROAD

WALL FARM

DOWN STEPS AND PATH TO STILE

SWILLETTS FARM

FROM STEEP FIELD

COURTWOOD FARM

NEWNHAM

TO PILSDON

N.T. STILES

F/P AND W/R (s)

OPEN ACCESS

O.S. TRIG POINT. 911 FT.

ROAD

WESSEX RIDGEWAY

PILSDON PEN

12 - PILSDON PEN AND LEWESDON HILL

INFORMATION AND VIEWS FROM PILSDON PEN

WILLIAM WORDSWORTH:

Having said that Pilsdon Pen contains 7.3/4 acres and that, in Hutchin's time, a trigonometrical survey placed Pilsdon Pen second to Lewesdon Hill at 934 ft and 960 ft respectively, let's move onto a connection with the Lake District which is worthy of a book about the equivalent of three Scafell Pikes.

South-West of Pilsdon Pen, near Bettiscombe, stood Racedown Lodge.   Wordsworth first met Samuel Taylor Coleridge at the home of a rich sugar merchant in Bristol. This Mr Pinney owned Racedown Lodge and William and sister Dorothy rented it from him between September 1795 and June 1797.   This was in a depressed period in Wordsworth's life and it was here that he wrote the critically un-acclaimed tragedy 'The Borderers'.   It was also from Racedown Lodge that he wrote his one and only letter to the newspapers.   This was to the 'Sherborne Weekly Entertainer' in defence of Fletcher Christian after the mutiny on 'The Bounty'.   After all, they had been at school together in Cockermouth.   In June 1797, Coleridge joined William and Dorothy and they decided to leave Dorset and go to Nether Stowey in Somerset from whence, after just one year, they all returned to Lakeland, nevermore to visit Dorset.

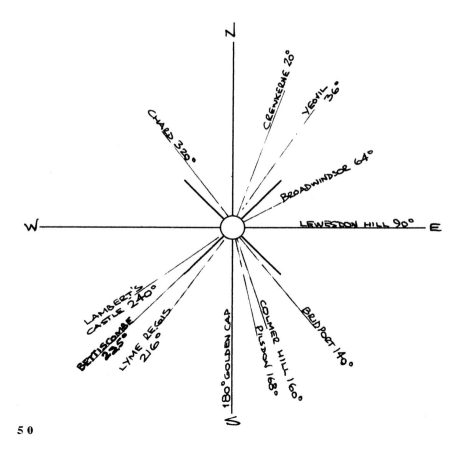

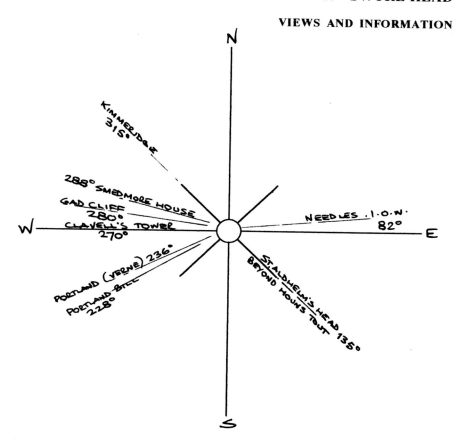

KIMMERIDGE:

The pretty stone and thatch village lies a good 3/4 mile from the crumbling cliffs and its little church is a delight.   St Nicholas' is very small, very old and built of rubble limestone.   It still has its original 12thC nave and its Norman South porch.   The bellcote and buttresses were added to the West end in the 15thC and it was extensively rebuilt in 1872.   The bituminous shale from the cliffs provided a jet-like stone which was treasured by the Romans who used it to fashion beautiful jewellery - much of which is exhibited in local museums.   The turnings from the jewellers lathes are known locally as coal money.   Clavell's Tower was built by Rev John Richards who assumed the name of Clavell on inheriting Smedmore House in 1817.   His ancestor, Sir William Clavell tried to extract alum from the shale and also to emulate the Romans who had extracted oil from the shale to boil sea water to extract salt.   He managed to sell some of this oil to a customer in Paris but the fuel burnt with such a horrid smell, that this venture failed as well.

Sir William Clavell built Smedmore House in the 17thC but it was entirely remodelled in the early 18thC when the South Front was added by Sir Christopher Wren.

O.S. MAP NO. 195   REFERENCE SY 933785

Swyre Head is the highest peak on the Isle of Purbeck. It is easily reached from the hilltop village of Kingston but it is best tackled from Kimmeridge Bay car park. Kimmeridge lies 4 miles West-South-West of Corfe Castle on the A351 Wareham to Swanage road and only local bus 275 goes there - and then only on Thursdays. This journey starts with an exciting clifftop walk and ends with a rewarding 400 ft final assault of Swyre Head. The return is a pleasant, descending stroll along Smedmore Hill and across level fields to the car park.

From the car park, follow the cliff edge through a second car park to the lane which leads down to wooden huts and the sea. From the 'Coast Path' signpost, follow this lane down for 100 yards and then turn left up the steep steps by another 'Coast Path' sign. Through bushes and alongside a LH fence, you reach the clifftop by Clavell's Tower. Past the tower and the 'Chapmans Pool 3.3/4' sign, keep to the footpath, hugging the barbed-wire fence as necessary. It's better than getting too close to the cliff edge as it is seriously unstable. Just follow the path, admiring the view and taking care until you reach a stone at Rope Head Lake labelled 'Kimmeridge Bay 1.1/2. Chapmans Pool 2.1/4' so keep your eyes off the book until then.

Go over the stile at Rope Head Lake and follow the undulating LH bank and hedge as it climbs up the field to the stile with a Coast Path direction stone on its other side. Go over the stile and meander through a square enclosure with a track to the left which heads down to Swalland Farm. From here, you have a final 400 ft climb to the top, so join the track on the far side of the enclosure and follow it up to an opening with another track turning off to the left. Keep straight on up into a widening, bumpy field of rough grass. Keep straight up Smedmore Hill on a thin, bending path through gorse bushes to the top Footpath-arrowed stile - stopping as often as you need en route. Over the stile, turn right and go over the last stile onto the end of the ridge around the barrow on Swyre Head. Enjoy the wonderful views over the farmland and the coast and then go back over the stile to start your ridge walk to Kimmeridge.

Keeping near to the LH wall, go through the Bridleway-arrowed gate and cross the next field to another half-gate which leads you onto a fence-enclosed, rutted track. There isn't any danger this time, but don't look at the book until you near the end of the descending ridge. Just enjoy the 3/4 mile of gentle strolling and the fine views.

After a sweeping, scrub and gorse-packed LH bend, you reach a tarmac lane. Turn left and walk down to a T-junction. Cross over, just downhill from a pair of gates with a 'Tyneham' pointer, and go over the stile which is signposted 'Kimmeridge 1/4'. Go down the steep, grassy slopes and through the gate onto the path past St Nicholas' Church. Down the steps at the other end, follow the road down, past the RH playing fields and the LH Post Office/Tea Rooms and straight through the village. When the cottages finish on the right, go over the Footpath-arrowed stile into the first field.

Follow the RH edge of the field (garden on right) down to cross a hedge-clad stream by a bridge with a stile on either end. Turn left and follow the stream-side path along the bottom edge of three fields which are divided by hedges and stiles, each with a derelict stone barn to the right of the stile. Go through the last Footpath-arrowed gate onto the Oil Extraction road and turn left. Go through the barrier and past the W.C. on your way back to the car park at the end of a wonderfully varied walk.

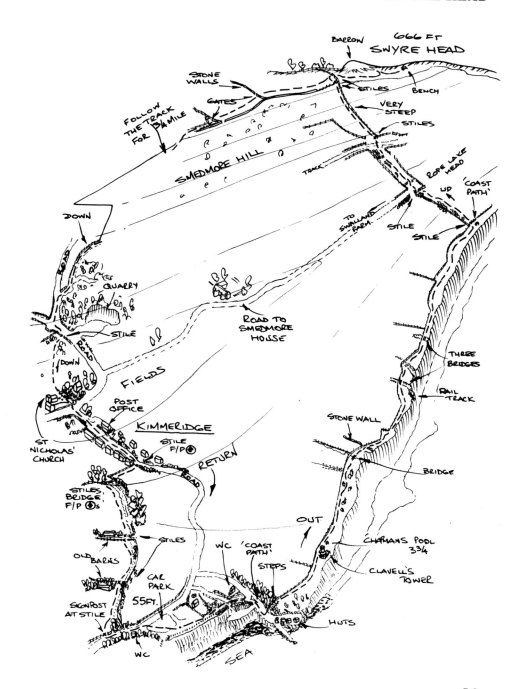

666 FT
SWYRE HEAD

BARROW

STONE WALLS
GATES
FOLLOW THE TRACK FOR 3/4 MILE

STILES
BENCH
VERY STEEP
STILES

SMEDMORE HILL

TRACK

ROPE LAKE HEAD
UP
'COAST PATH'

DOWN

TO SWALLAND FARM
STILE
STILE

QUARRY

ROAD TO SMEDMORE HOUSE

STILE

THREE BRIDGES

DOWN

FIELDS

RAIL TRACK

POST OFFICE

KIMMERIDGE

STONE WALL

STILE F/P

RETURN

BRIDGE

ST NICHOLAS' CHURCH

STILES BRIDGE F/P s

STILES

OLD BARNS

WC

'COAST PATH'

OUT

CHAPMANS POOL 33/4

CLAVELL'S TOWER

STEPS

CAR PARK

55 FT.

SIGNPOST AT STILE

HUTS

WC

SEA

O.S. MAP NO. 194   REFERENCE SY 716843/713845

Sutton Poyntz lies 1 mile North of the A353 Weymouth to Warmwell road and the Southern National bus A runs there infrequently.   Other than that, you'll need a car or bike to get to the starting point by the duck-pond opposite 'The Springhead'. After a stroll through the village and across a long field, there is an unremitting haul up the tail end of the White Horse before you can enjoy a fine ridge walk to the O. S. trig point at East Hill and a superb return down the ridge paths to Sutton Poyntz.

Set off from the duck-pond, walking upstream and past the pub's parking area on the edge of Mission Hall Lane.   The lane bends right at the entrance to the Waterworks and, between houses and a single industrial unit on your left, it leads to a gate which is marked 'Footpath Only. No Horses'.   Go through the gate onto a short, enclosed track between wide verges.   Through the squeeze stile by the next gate, you will be in a very long and wide field which slopes up to your left towards the chalk escarpment of White Horse Hill.   A finger-post points to three Footpaths but the diagonal one across this field probably isn't visible.   Don't worry about it!   Just follow the track straight ahead, next to the RH hedge, and a diagonal path will be cut through later on.

On the way along this track, look out for the White Horse.   It looks a little distorted from here - something like I have shown on the map.   When you find the path cut across the wide, upward sloping field, follow it to a stile in the deep bushes in the top corner.   The Footpath arrow points straight up the hill.   So, gird up your loins and begin to climb up the very steep path through high scrub and elderberry bushes with a fence not far to your left.   Frequent stops may be permitted.   Out of the bushes, you will find rough steps in the long grass.   If you cut across to the Horse's tail, you'll see just how big it is.   I couldn't climb the length of his tail without stopping - but then, I was probably having a bad day.   Through gorse near the top of the ridge, you emerge onto a clearer slope.   Head over to the LH fence but keep going up on the path until it leads you actually over a round barrow.   Down the other side, go through the left gate in the fence, signed 'Inland Coast Path. Bincombe. Abbotsbury'.

A rising track runs between a RH fence and two more barrows on the left.   Between these two, you will find the East Hill O.S. trig point from where there are far ranging views.   Dragging yourself away, rejoin the track and follow it to an exit onto a chalk track which runs the other side of the RH hedge with an Inland Coast Path signpost - but don't leave this field.   Go past a LH Footpath next to a round barrow and keep the hedge between you and the track for about 200 yards.   Past a gate with another Inland Coast Path signpost and another round barrow, join a track which comes from the chalk track behind the RH hedge and runs left, past the ruins of Northdown Barn. This track soon swings right, through a gate with an Inland Coast Path arrow onto a rising grassy shelf track with a fence on your right and the scarp on your left.

Before the track bears round to the right, before the top of the rise, turn onto a smaller, peaty path without any signs.   This runs level for a few yards through gorse and brambles.   When it forks, take the LH fork - aiming for Weymouth beach.   Keep descending until you meet a wider track T-junction by a grassy mound with a seat on top.   Turn left and follow the chalky track down to the Waterworks track at the bottom.   Turn right over a stile by a gate onto the level track.   Follow it, over another stile by a gate and, alongside the iron-fenced waterworks, through a field and back into the village - arriving on the other side of the duckpond.

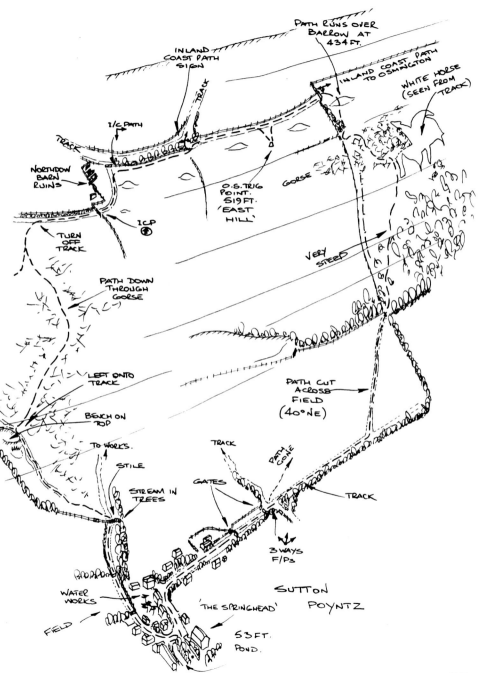

PATH RUNS OVER BARROW AT 434 FT.

INLAND COAST PATH TO OSMINGTON

INLAND COAST PATH SIGN

WHITE HORSE (SEEN FROM TRACK)

TRACK

I/C PATH

TRACK

NORTHDOW BARN RUINS

GORSE

O.S. TRIG POINT. 519 FT. 'EAST HILL'

ICP

TURN OFF TRACK

VERY STEEP

PATH DOWN THROUGH GORSE

LEFT ONTO TRACK

PATH CUT ACROSS FIELD (40°NE)

BENCH ON TOP

TO WORKS.

STILE

TRACK

STREAM IN TREES

GATES

PATH GONE

TRACK

3 WAYS F/Ps

WATER WORKS

SUTTON POYNTZ

'THE SPRINGHEAD'

FIELD

53 FT. POND.

14 - WHITE HORSE HILL AND EAST HILL

INFORMATION AND VIEWS FROM EAST HILL

SUTTON POYNTZ:

In the Domesday Book as Sutone and Sudtone, the first part of the village's name means 'South Town'. The Poyntz family were ancient landowners and lords of the vills of Sutton and neighbouring Preston (meaning 'Priest's Town' because of its relation to the church of Salisbury). In the time of Edward II, Sir Nicholas Poyntz gave Preston in marriage with his daughter Margaret to Sir John de Newburgh (of local Winfrith Newburgh).

From the productive chalk downs, many clear springs gush forth and, by the time the spring water has passed Springhead and reached Preston, it has earned the title of River Jordan.

WHITE HORSE HILL:

The famous White Horse is thought to be considerably older than the time when King George III first visited Weymouth in 1789 and added an air of respectability to the 'seaside resort'. The figure on the horse is definitely George but the equestrian edifice is believed to be as ancient as the Westbury or Uffington white horses.

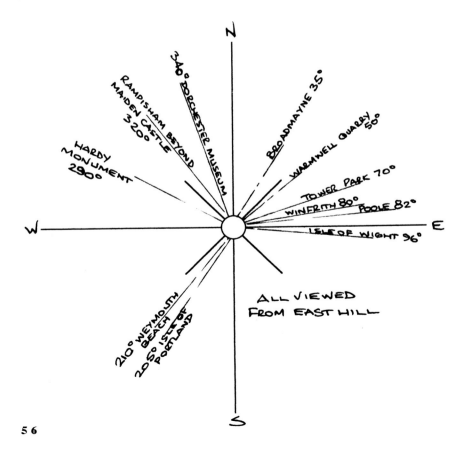

VIEWS AND INFORMATION

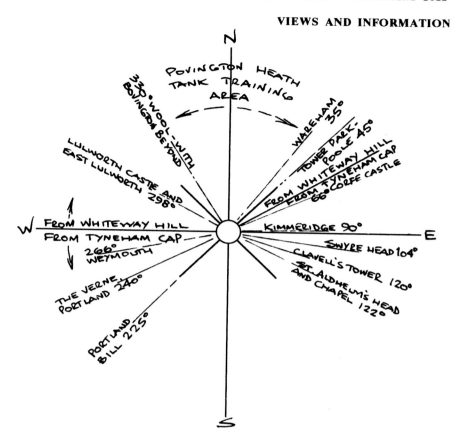

TYNEHAM:

In the Domesday Book, Tyneham was divided into four parcels.   Two were called Tigeham and two were called Tingeham and there were four owners.   St Mary's Church is an 'ancient but very small edifice, repaired 1744" - and since then,but the Rev Hutchins wouldn't have known about it.   Tyneham House was the seat of the Rev John Bond in 1820 and it was this family who gave their name to Bond Street in London.   The Elizabethan Manor House was finished, as proclaimed by a date stone, in 1583 although part of the same construction bears an earlier date - 1567.   Mrs L M G Bond, who was evacuated from the Manor House for the War effort, has written an excellent book evoking the spirit of old Tyneham.   It is called 'Tyneham' and was published by Longmans, late of Dorchester.

WHITEWAY HILL:

Hutchins only reference to the nomenclature of this spot (in 1773 remember) is "from a conspicuous white road or way leading over the chalk hill from Lulworth to Tyneham".   This is the very same way which is used on this walk to come back down the hill into the village.

15 - WHITEWAY HILL AND TYNEHAM CAP   608 FT/530 FT

O.S. MAP NO. 194   REFERENCE SY 876809/892797

Tyneham deserted village is tucked away near the Dorset coast in the depths of the Isle of Purbeck.   It is best approached from the A351 Wareham by-pass, turning off to go through Creech .   Taken over by the military during World War II, the villagers of Tyneham had to leave and they haven't been allowed to return as the whole area is still used for army training and firing practice.   As a result, the area is rich in wildlife and is largely unspoilt whilst the cottages, the school and the rectory in the village have fallen into romantic ruin.   The scenery is second to none and the walks along grassy clifftops offer delicious views of an incomparable coastline.   The Range Walks are open at weekends all year and in the week during the summer holidays.   To be doubly sure, you can check with the Gunnery School on 01929-462721 Ext. 4819.

STAGE 1 - TYNEHAM CAP

Starting in Tyneham car park, leave by the gate at the far end of the car park and cross the stream through the woods.   Where the stone sign points right for 'Worbarrow Bay 2/3' go straight across and over the stile by the cattle grid.   The clear gravel track leads into an M.O.D. target area so make sure you follow the yellow post-marked Footpath as it zig-zags up the long slopes to Gad Cliff.   The track doubles back at a bend with a tremendous view into Worbarrow Bay and then continues up to a stile in a wire fence.   Over the stile, turn sharp right (between the posts) alongside the fence to join the clifftop path which comes up from Worbarrow over another stile nearer the cliff edge.   Turn left on the path but, if you dare, have a very cautious peek over the cliff edge.   Be warned, erosion of the underlying Kimmeridge Clays and Portland Sand has caused falls of Portland Stone and Purbeck material.   It is still quite unstable and overhangs a terrific drop to the rocks below.

Follow the grassy path just below the cliff edge and enjoy the views unfolding along the valley towards Corfe Castle and along the coast.   When you reach a stile with a 'forbidden' track through a gateway in the stone wall just beyond it, go over and drop down to a luxurious stone bench which is sheltered from the breezes and has a beautiful view.   From the seat, the paths divide.   The RH fork leads down and round Tyneham Cap to Kimmeridge Bay, the oil well and the car park.   Take the LH fork, rising slightly through the grass.   After about 200 yards, you meet the track coming back out from the 'forbidden' field on your left.   Keep straight on up the grass and stony track, much clearer and wider now with a stone wall on your left, to the top of the hill.   This is Tyneham Cap and, before you begin the walk to Worbarrow Bay and Whiteway Hill, enjoy the superb views along the Purbeck Coast to your left and to towards Portland on your right.   Then, return to the junction of paths at Gad Cliff.

Go over the stile and begin a long, easy descent between the nearby cliff edge and the wire fences to Worbarrow Bay.   Near the end, the angle of the stone beds which you can see on Worbarrow Tout explains graphically why the hills slopes the way they do - and the pattern is repeated on the other side of Worbarrow Bay when you climb up to Flower's Barrow Hill Fort.   At the bottom, go through the kissing gate and walk over to the Information plinth for details of the lost village of Worbarrow.   Then , after a suitable rest to enjoy the seaside, drop down to cross the West branch of the valley track.   Passing a few, scarcely visible ruins of the stone village cottages, carry on down to the stream bridge and go up the other side, passing through the wire fence, continuing up the slope on the cliff path and climbing over a stile on the way.

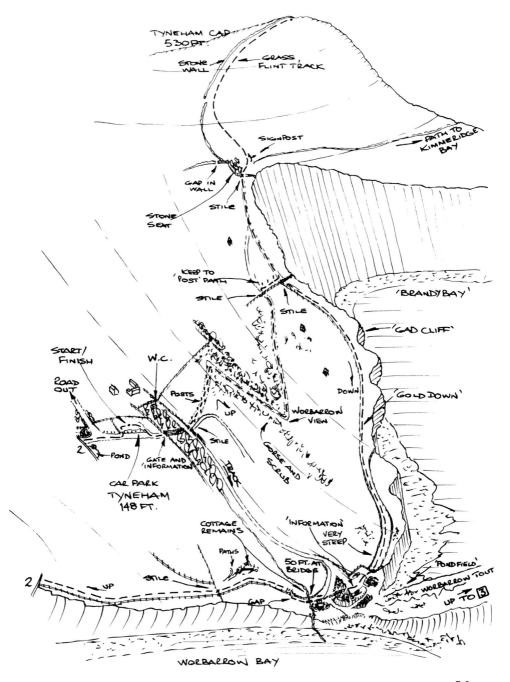

WORBARROW BAY

59

There are a few more sad ruins of village cottages whilst the climb is still a relatively easy stroll.   Buy the Tyneham Trail leaflet from the church when you get back and it will tell you who lived in these cottages.   It's all rather sad to think of this little community being broken up and removed from their home soil.

Keep on climbing and go over the next stile by the 'No. 1' target.   Now, be careful to bear left off the obvious grass track for a few yards so that you keep within the yellow marker posts.   Then rejoin the straight line ascent and go up and over a high ridge with a gun post over on your left.   Whether this ridge marks a supply track to the gun post or whether it, together with the banks and ditches all over this hill, is one of the earthworks connected with the Celtic fields all around Tyneham, I am not certain.

From here, the gorse seems to disappear whilst the hillside becomes really steep with some steps cut into it by thousands of walkers' feet over the years.   The valley between the two ridges you are tackling today runs through Wealden beds of clay, sand and grit but, as you climb up here, you are walking over beds of Greensand which lie between the Wealden and the chalk which forms the bulk of this ridge.   Where the steepest climb starts - that's where the greensand ends and the chalk begins.   This is an excellent substitute for climbing Scafell Pike and frequent pauses are not only allowed but highly recommended.

Eventually, you arrive at a stile in the top fence which borders Flower's Barrow with another gun post over to your left.   Over the stile, cross the defensive ditch into the Iron Age hill fort.   There are lovely views Northward from here but they get better when you leave to stroll along the top ridge of Rings Hill.   Nearly half of the hill fort has been claimed by the sea through cliff falls - most of which had already gone by 1744.   The Coast Path milestone points left to 'Lulworth Cove 2.1/2' and back down to 'Worbarrow Bay 3/4' - much of the latter being nearly vertical.   Leave the inner sanctum by turning right and going through the yellow post-marked exit through the ring and onto a level grassy path.

Enjoy this long, slightly downhill stroll before going over a stile and continuing slightly uphill with glorious views all around.   You soon arrive at 'No. 7' target and, shortly after that, the O.S. trig point for Whiteway Hill at 608 ft (with Firing Point B on your right - not a good place to be during gunnery practice).   With Povington Hill looming ahead at 630 ft, keep straight on down the path.   When you reach a stile and gate leading into a chalk track area with the road and its hairpin down to your left, go over the stile and follow the chalk track's sharp bend round to the right, clockwise around the flag-bedecked corner.   The milestone opposite points down to 'Tyneham 1'.   Enjoy the surprisingly steep chalk 'White Way' with lovely views en route for the whole mile back to Tyneham village.

After the stile at the bottom, follow the track around St Mary's churchyard and, past the old oak tree, planted to 'comemerate' (their spelling, not mine) the Coronation of George V in 1911.   Perhaps you could spend some time exploring the remains of the empty village before going home, putting your feet up and remembering all of the exciting and wonderful moments of this glorious walk.

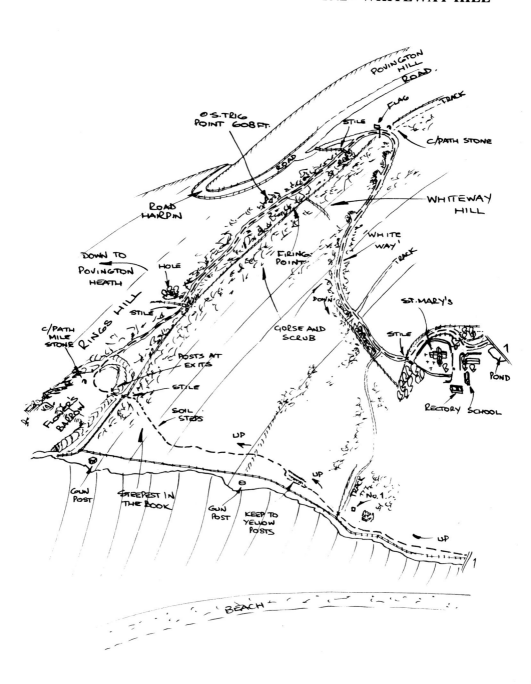

POVINGTON HILL ROAD.

TRACK

FLAG

STILE

C/PATH STONE

O.S.TRIG POINT 608FT.

ROAD

WHITEWAY HILL

ROAD HAIRPIN

WHITE WAY

TRACK

DOWN TO POVINGTON HEATH

HOLE

FIRING POINT

DOWN'

ST. MARY'S

STILE

RINGS HILL

STILE

C/PATH MILE STONE

GORSE AND SCRUB

STILE

POND

POSTS AT EXITS

RECTORY SCHOOL

FLOWER'S BARROW

STILE

SOIL STEPS

UP

UP

GUN POST

STEEPEST IN THE BOOK

GUN POST

KEEP TO YELLOW POSTS

TRACK No. 1.

UP

BEACH

INDEX